Dok Suni

Dok Suni

RECIPES FROM MY MOTHER'S KOREAN KITCHEN

또순이

Jenny Kwak

with Liz Fried

St. Martin's Press ❧ New York

THIS BOOK IS DEDICATED TO

THE WOMAN I ADMIRE MOST,

MY MOTHER.

IN MEMORY OF MICHAEL DARCY

DOK SUNI. Copyright © 1998 by Jenny Kwak. All rights reserved. Printed in the United States of America. No part of this book may be used or reproduced in any manner whatsoever without written permission except in the case of brief quotations embodied in critical articles or reviews. For information, address St. Martin's Press, 175 Fifth Avenue, New York, N.Y. 10010.

Book design by Songhee Kim

Library of Congress Cataloging-in-Publication Data

Kwak, Jenny.
    Dok Suni : recipes from my mother's Korean kitchen /
Jenny Kwak with Liz Fried.
      p. cm.
    Includes index.
    ISBN 0-312-19261-4
    1. Cookery, Korean.   2. Dok Suni's (Restaurant : New York, N.Y.)
I. Fried, Liz.   II. Title.
TX724.5.K65K83   1998
641.59519—DC21   98-18718
                                          CIP

10 9 8 7 6 5 4

Contents

Acknowledgments

Many thanks to my friend and literary agent Jessica Wainwright, my co-writer Liz Fried, my editor Marian Lizzi at St. Martin's, Adam Campanella for his exceptional work with the photographs, and Jennifer Udell and Dolores Cluster for being such gracious food stylists: this book would not have been possible without their dedication.

I would like to express my gratitude to the women who work so hard with my mother in the kitchen. Thank you Bok Sook Kang, Hee Ran Park, Bei Young Heang, and Ji Song Ja for your patience, insight, and answers to my questions on Korean food.

And my devoted friends who supported Dok Suni's, thank you Sehti Na, Tom Clapp, Jenna Na, Corina Prados, Helen Kim, Christine Park, Kimberly Bliss, Claude De Castro, Darrin Amellio, Butch Belair, Jerome Duran, Justin Guip, John Lurie, and Alex Rockwell for all the good advice, friendship and faith you have shown me throughout the years.

And I would like to thank my father and my sisters, Moon Sun and Jane, for their love and encouragement always.

Introduction

In the seventeen years we've spent in the United States, not a day has gone by that we haven't eaten Korean food—thanks to my mother. Finding a Korean food market is much easier now, but when we first arrived, my mother did most of her shopping at American supermarkets. She could find almost everything there. And from the Korean market, she bought rib eye meats, tofu, and Korean condiments like sesame oil and chili pepper flakes for her pantry. Her dishes were adjusted to what was available here, but she never compromised when it came to good ingredients.

The kitchen was my mother's territory and a common haven—she didn't have to know how to speak English to appreciate the art of cooking. She kept her kitchen in an orderly fashion, organized for her convenience. She liked shopping for kitchenware that would make her work easier, and she utilized two ample-size refrigerators because one just could not hold all the food. She watched American cooking shows regularly, and when she felt like venturing into something different, she'd make salads for pita bread, burgers, or steak. Her hamburgers were delicious. (When she seasoned ground beef for burgers, she couldn't help but embellish it with some Korean flair.) She would freeze about two dozen patties in the refrigerator at a time and among the three of us they wouldn't even last a week.

As long as I can remember, our extended family of four households have relished her food. Whenever my mother prepares her "seasonal" kimchi, she pickles plenty to divide among the households. Regularly, my mother visited her older sister. She would take a portion of beef marinade, salted fish, or other Korean delicacies. Her sister and family raved about the food and would ask when my mother would make it again. After a long day of playing in the sun, I remember that there was nothing better than coming home to eat food that my mother prepared. After school, there was nothing more nourishing. When we got sick, nothing healed us as fast as her soups, not even medicine. When we were being punished, we'd stay locked away in our room until she called for us to come out and eat. When we were having problems with our school work, she'd sit us down to have a snack before we went back to studying.

With food, our mother kept us full, leaving us to concentrate on the other important things in our lives. My sisters and I never missed a chance to better ourselves. My mother did everything to provide for us, and there was no excuse not to succeed in life. Now I see that there was nothing more important to her than teaching her children to be independent and strong.

I remember the moment we were trying to come up with a name for our restaurant. Dok Suni—the phrase describes a strong woman of any age, resilient and fearless. A woman of endurance. I realized then that this was how my mother perceived herself. And since that day, my views on what it means to be my mother's daughter changed entirely.

As a working woman, the owner of a restaurant, and its chef, my mother began to discover easy and effective ways to cook Korean food. For good Korean food, preparation is key, especially when making a soup or stew with beef. Ginger, rice wine, or a boiling process are used to help eliminate excess fat and the odor in the meat. Kiwi is used as a good tenderizer for beef. Garlic and onion are used in a juice consistency to season more evenly. Staying true to the essence of the flavor in every ingredient makes for a wholesome and delicious dish, and knowing how to do that is what makes my mother a great cook.

In recent years, Korean food has become very popular among my friends, and other Americans looking for delicious ways to cook and eat.

There is something to satisfy everyone. Those who love spices like to indulge in dishes such as ojinx-o bokum (squid sauté) and d'ak-dori-tang (stewed chicken). For those needing a healthy pick-me-up, try bibimbop (a rice and vegetable medley). Korean soups like miyok-gook (seaweed soup) and samgae-tang (ginseng chicken soup) help to revitalize you if you're feeling run down or sick. And if you are throwing a party, a real crowd pleaser is the seafood pancake with a chilled bottle of soju (Korean vodka).

With our cookbook, my mom, my sisters, and I hope to introduce you to Korean home cooking. I also hope to provide you with recipes for many of the delicious dishes I grew up with. Most of all, I'd like to share with you the richness of my culture. As my mother would say to our guests and family members, "Enjoy and eat plenty!"

맛있게 많이 드세요!

(pronounced: Matshikgay moni dēsey yo!)

—Jenny Kwak

Mom's Shopping List

엄마의 장보기

Beef Stock (dashida)

Dashida is a beef-flavored stock used very modestly in Korean cooking. It is not always necessary to use dashida when recipes call for it—any beef, chicken, or vegetable stock can be used in substitution. Just remember, the flavor can be significantly different without the use of stock.

Cheong-Po

Cheong-po is like tofu and it is made with mung beans instead of soybeans. It can be found in a Korean market by the tofu. Cheong-po can be seasoned with soy sauce and sesame oil to make a tasty side dish. It is also delicious in the bibimbop, as shown on the cover.

Chicken (d'ak)

Chicken is usually prepared whole, as chicken cubes, chunks, and shreds. Korean markets carry popular American brands of chicken.

Chives (buchu)

Chives are important to Korean cuisine, especially in dishes that call for pickling. They are basically used fresh and uncooked.

Chrysanthemum Leaves (sook-gat)

These leaves, like perilla, have a unique flavor. Eaten fresh, seasoned, or blanched, *sook-gat* taste bitter but are very refreshing. They are usually sold in bundles in the produce section of Korean markets.

Dried Persimmons (gam)

Persimmons are often the edible treats of the New Year and Christmas. Often mentioned in many old Korean folktales, they've been a treat for centuries.

My sister Moon Sun especially likes persimmons. She had a tendency to *gam chuh* fruit, which means to squirrel away. We would always tease her about this when she was little. When the fruit was set out after dinner, the family would gather around and eat it together. Moon Sun, however, always picked out the choicest pieces of fruit and scurried away to her bedroom. With persimmons, she would pick the softest, most orange ones. We often joked that she treated herself like a little princess.

Dried persimmons are sweet with a chewy texture like candy, and are quite a contrast to fresh persimmons, which are fleshy and very juicy. My mother used dried persimmons as garnish in sujong-gwa, a punch that is supposed to sustain health and well-being.

Duakuan

Duakuan is radish pickled in vinegar. It is yellow in color and sold in plastic packages in the frozen-food section in any Korean or Japanese market. Duakuan has a sweet flavor and is one of the ingredients to make kimbop, a seaweed roll of rice and vegetable.

Eggplant (gagi)

My mother prefers the Chinese eggplant, a slimmer version of the Western eggplant. It can be found in Chinatown and in most Korean markets. They can also be found dried and packaged, but using fresh eggplant is better if at all possible.

Garlic and Onions

Fresh onions and garlic are easy to buy anywhere. When recipes call for crushed garlic, finely chop it until the consistency is even.

If the recipe calls for garlic or onion juice, use a blender. Avoid diluting the potency by adding too much water when liquefying. Add a little water, just enough to help the blender mix smoothly. For the onion, shift the juice in a mesh strainer for a smooth consistency before using in recipes.

Gingerroot (seng-gang)

Gingerroot is an important flavoring, commonly used with garlic. It is a pale brown and gnarled tuber with a leathery skin. Its flesh has a strong citrus smell. Gingerroot, like sesame oil, is considered good for the body. It should be used in minimal quantities as its flavor is very strong. Gingerroot comes ground and minced in most Asian markets, and fresh gingerroot is available in most produce markets. When I was young, I could appreciate the taste of ginger and even ate it raw. Little bits of it were in my mother's pickled recipes and sometimes I would bite into a piece of ginger when eating kimchi. It was strange for my palate and I couldn't help but scrunch up my face in distaste the first few times I tried it. This display always made my mother laugh.

To use ginger for the recipe measurements, just finely mince and grind using the blunt edge of your knife.

Ginseng Root (in-sam)

Ginseng root can be found at any specialty food store or Asian market. Koreans love ginseng for its medicinal qualities and use it to cook with. It is an important ingredient in the traditional Korean soup. Remember to use ginseng in small amounts since this herb is very bitter.

Hot Mustard (ghea-ja)

Hot mustard usually appears as a paste in Korean markets. It is also sold ground into a fine yellow brown powder. My mother prefers to buy powder to whip up her own sauce. Similar to the Japanese horseradish wasabi, it is lethally spicy. It clears a stuffy nose and sinuses instantly. Hot mustard can be used in salad dressings and in cold noodle soups.

To make your own mustard sauce: boil ½ cup water. Let it cool for 5 minutes. Combine the water with ½ cup hot mustard powder. Using a spoon, stir together. The more you stir, the hotter the sauce will get. My mother whips this creamy sauce together until she feels a sting from just one whiff.

Kirby Cucumbers (oye)

Cucumbers are used in many Korean dishes. In my home, they were always around in the kitchen, and we often heard the quick thud of my mother's knife as she sectioned them on the cutting board. Cucumbers are firm and at the same time saturated in water. Kirby cucumbers are easily found in American markets and have many uses in preparing Korean food. However, the cucumbers sold at Korean markets are a bit different and better to use. The difference is not readily apparent. These cucumbers are slimmer, have less water, and are better for pickling to make kimchi than the Kirby cucumbers. Yet both are fine to use.

Korean Flour (milga-rue)

There are several types of Korean flour. Although the ingredients are the same as in most Western flours, Korean flour has a different texture. It is very fine, starchlike. It is easier to work with and it retains moisture better than domestic flour. However, my first dumpling-making experience involved working with Western flour to make the dough skins and it turned out fine.

Be careful not to confuse wheat flours with some of the other cooking flours or powder batters available in Korean markets. There are flat cake (*buchim*) breading and frying flours. These flours are often mixtures and have flavorings such as MSG.

Meats (*gogi*)

The variety of ways beef is prepared is essential to Korean cuisine. A major factor in taste and flavor rests on the cut of the meat. For dishes like kalbi and bulgogi, the rib meat is used. Kalbi is prepared using short rib meat and each slice is approximately ¼-inch thick, including the rib bone. Bulgogi meat is the sliced rib eye of beef. It is usually ⅛-inch thick. For both dishes, look for lean meat with very few fat deposits. This is important since there will be very little to enjoy when the fat melts away upon cooking. All large Korean supermarkets will offer packaged meat specifically for kalbi and bulgogi. If this is not available, ask the local butcher to slice the meat according to the above measurements.

For soy sauce beef and yuke-jaong, a popular scorching hot beef soup, look for flank steak or beef brisket. This meat has a definite grain streak that shreds very easily. Again, look for the leanest meat.

For beef to use in salads or cold noodle soups, look for beef shank, otherwise known as beef satay in Asian markets. This beef tends to be tender when boiled and it is mouth watering when prepared in salads and soups.

A rich milky broth called *suhllun-tang* is made from boiling the bone marrow. This soup is prized by Koreans in the wintertime. The broth is not only hearty and soothing, but also a panacea for the weak and ailing. Korean and American markets alike offer bone marrow in packages.

Mushrooms (*buh-suhhut*)

My mother always cooked with plenty of mushrooms because she knew we liked them, whether grilled with bulgogi, stewed, or in a sauté. She usually used mushrooms found in American markets including fresh oyster mushrooms. Other recipes that called for particular mushrooms like dried mushroom, the paghot or black mushrooms—often referred to as cloud ears or wood ears—can be found in the dried-goods section of the market.

Napa Cabbage (baechu)

A trip to an Asian market will offer you a bounty of napa cabbage, also known as Korean or Chinese cabbage. It is a pale cabbage, whose leafy part ranges from an almost white green to something approaching a celery color. Napa cabbage is the most common to use to make kimchi, which is best described as spicy pickled cabbage. It is not as dry and stiff as white and red cabbage; the texture is more watery like endive, but not bitter. Look for baechu that is crisp and unspeckled around the stem. The leafy part should also be firm.

Noodles (gook-su)

There are many types of noodles used in traditional Korean cuisine; however in this book, we use three basic kinds. They are noodles made from potato starch, buckwheat, or wheat flour. Potato noodles appear in japchae, a noodle and vegetable sauté, and in yuke-jaong. Whenever my mother made yuke-jaong, the clear noodles always sank to the bottom. These noodles are very light and colorless when cooked.

Buckwheat noodles are very common in cold noodle dishes and salads. These noodles are light brown in color. Wheat flour noodles are usually used in cold dishes too. In the cold noodle soup called nyeng-myun, buckwheat or wheat flour noodles can be used.

Although it is best to look for these noodles in Korean markets, similar noodles can be found in other Asian markets. Look on the back of the package for the ingredients list, as some noodles come in varying mixtures of buckwheat and wheat. The noodles are also referred to as Korean or Oriental vermicelli. Buckwheat and wheat flour noodles can be found in the refrigerated section of markets, near the egg-skin dumpling wrappers.

Peppers (goit-chu)

Koreans use the long green chili peppers to cook with, but they also eat them raw with a dipping sauce, either soybean sauce or red pepper sauce. These long green chili peppers are easy to find in Korean and American markets alike. Use them for recipes that call for spicy green chili peppers.

If for some reason you can't find them, jalapeño peppers make a fine substitution.

My mother and I used to pick out the choicest pepper from the mounds of the chili peppers in the market's bins. The firm, dark green peppers were usually the hottest. Sometimes my mother would break open a pepper to see if the seeds were fresh and white. At the dinner table, we always left the dark greens ones for our parents to eat.

Another pepper used in Korean cooking is the twist pepper, or gwari. It is 1½ to 2 inches long, with a wrinkled texture on the outside. These peppers are mild in flavor and very tasty pickled with soy sauce or used in sautés. Look for twist peppers at a Korean market. They are perfect in any dish that calls for a mild pepper.

Perilla Leaves (quen-neep)

Perilla leaves have a very distinct mintlike smell. Fresh perilla leaves are used to accompany bulgogi, Korean beef marinade barbecue. They are found in Korean markets in small bundles. When I was growing up, many neighbors grew perilla leaves in their backyards. The leaves are also seasoned and served as a side dish prepared by wrapping individual leaves around rice.

Radish (moo)

Radish is used in almost everything and we prepare it in a variety of ways. Its uses run the gamut from raw, softened in soups and stews, or pickled as a preserve. Korean markets offer whole radishes, usually found in the produce section by the leafy greens or by the roots and bulbs. It is called radish or giant white radish. Be careful not to confuse it with daikon or turnips since all are in the same size range, and don't use Western red radishes as a substitute.

Red Dates (dae-chu)

Red dates are one of the prized exports of Korea. Usually sold dried in Korean markets, they are added to mixtures of grains. My father, when cooking, loves to add red dates to white rice just before steaming. The dates' sweet taste is also used in ginseng chicken soup.

Red Pepper Flakes and Red Pepper Powder (goit-chu garu)

The spicy agent in Korean cooking is the red chili pepper used in either a flake or powder form. Koreans do not consume the red chili pepper raw but it is added in small quantities as garnish. Mostly, the red chili pepper is dried and crushed to use as a seasoning condiment and it is the most important ingredient in making kimchi. Crushed coarsely, it is red pepper flakes; refined, it is red pepper powder. Most recipes call specifically for flakes or powder.

Red pepper flakes and powder are found in a Korean market. Cayenne pepper is not a recommended substitution for red pepper powder since it is mild in spiciness.

Red Pepper Sauce (goit-chu jang)

Red pepper sauce is a staple seasoning for many Korean dishes and it is made with red pepper paste. Red pepper paste, sometimes called "hot pepper paste" or "chili pepper paste" on the label, is easily found in any Korean or Asian market. It is sold by the jar or in plastic containers. My mother usually buys the big jars of red pepper paste and uses it for many months.

To make the red pepper sauce, combine 2 cups red pepper paste with ½ cup water, ½ cup vegetable oil, 2 tablespoons finely chopped garlic, and fry over a medium flame for 20 minutes stirring occasionally. Then, mix in 1 teaspoon sesame seeds. Store in a jar, refrigerated, and use it to cook with or serve it as a dipping sauce. It's great with fresh vegetables, fish, or barbecued beef, though we enjoy dunking sticks of fresh cucumber, peppers, steamed broccoli, little bundles of chrysanthemum, and perilla leaves into this sauce as well.

Rice (bop)

Korean rice is very similar to Japanese rice. It is usually medium grain and becomes glutinous when cooked. Although it is most common to see white rice in Korean homes and at restaurants, Koreans also enjoy mixtures of brown rice, beans, barley, and sweet rice. (Sweet rice is stickier and more glutinous than the medium grain rice and is used mostly in dishes with a mixture of grains or to make Korean pastries.) These items can easily be found in Korean and American markets. Rice is usually sold in large 50-pound bags or smaller 21-pound bags. A common brand: Kokuhorose—medium grain enriched without talc.

Rice Cakes (d'uk)

Rice cakes used in this book are found in Korean markets and in some Asian markets. There are also special *d'uk* houses in Korean neighborhoods where they make fresh rice cakes. At the food markets, there are two types of rice cakes to consider.

There are the sliced and slivered kind to make rice cake soup on occasions like New Year's Day. Sometimes you can find them in the frozen food section in plastic bags. These will feel hard because they're frozen and need to be thawed in cold water for 30 minutes before being used in soup.

Then there are rice cake logs used to make dukboki, a popular rice cake dish. In Korean markets, freshly made rice cakes are sold by the check-out counters along with breads and pastries. Buy a portion and try the spicy rice cake sauté on page 59. My mother sometimes warmed up leftover rice cake logs by steaming or boiling them, or sticking them in the microwave, and we'd eat them dipped in sesame oil. If she heated them in a frying pan with a little bit of oil, we'd sprinkle some sugar on too for a tasty sweet treat. You can't go wrong with rice cakes; they are delicious prepared any way.

Rice Vinegar (shik-cho)

Rice vinegar is most commonly used for the sour and the tangy taste in Korean cuisine. Rice vinegars are commonly found under Japanese labels. There is a versatile variety of Korean vinegar that is made from malt, sweet potatoes, apples, onions, brown rice, and persimmons. Look around the aisles near corn malt syrups and millet jellies, syrupy liquids used in lieu of refined sugars. Read the label for rice vinegar. Do not confuse rice vinegars with mirin, the Japanese sweet rice wine, as they are similar in color and consistency. Mirin is flavored and mildly sweet.

Roasted Corn and Barley Tea (bori-cha, oksusu-cha)

Roasted corn and barley tea is the equivalent of clean drinking water for native Koreans. It is usually prepared in the winter to fortify those who are unlucky enough to be outdoors for too long. One liter of water is boiled with enough barley and corn to completely cover the surface of the water. When it is clear, a light tan to brown in color, let it cool briefly and drink. It can also be chilled and served as a refreshment in the summer. Although it can be brewed darker and thus cloudier, the tea is more tasty with just a hint of the corn and barley.

Roasted corn and barley come packaged and are available in Korean markets in the tea or dried grains sections. Sometimes the teas are made using just corn or just barley. But it is a combination of the two that is supposed to make the tea a health drink. This is the way my mother always brewed it. Koreans drink this tea with meals to aid digestion and to complement spicy foods.

Salt (soogim)

Sea salt is a natural salt that comes in two forms, coarse or fine. It is not iodized, and is more flavorful than iodized salt. It is available in most markets. My mother buys the coarse salt found in the Korean markets. Look for sea salt in the aisles where the markets carry malt, millet, grains, and sugars. Specialty health food stores carry natural sea salt as well.

In Korea, there are sea salt farms that naturally cultivate the salt under the sun. Korean sea salt is unrefined and sometimes other particles from the sea are dried with the salt. These particles are not harmful—just remember to pick them out!

Seaweed (kim)

Seaweed is used in a variety of ways. It can be served as a side dish or be used in soups or to make rice rolls.

If you need seaweed for a side dish or making rice rolls with, look for the laver (thin sheets of seaweed) that comes in 8 × 8-inch pieces. For Korean dishes, flavored seaweed is not used. Read the package carefully before purchasing the seaweed to make sure no flavoring has been used.

To make kimbop, the rice and vegetable roll, use the 8 × 8-inch sheets of laver.

As a side dish, the seaweed is slightly toasted and salted and cut up in 2-inch squares. To make this, take the laver and slowly wisp it across a low flame. The laver should be thinner and crispier. Then flavor the seaweed by basting it lightly with vegetable oil using a brush. Sprinkle with fine salt and cut up the laver, keeping the seaweed in a pile. The toasted seaweed will keep if stored in an airtight container. Toasted seaweed is eaten with a scoop of rice on top. It can also be crumbled up for use as seasoning or garnish.

For soups use the seaweed that comes frozen or dried (called *wakame* in Japanese) as strands, pieces, or bits.

Sesame Oil (changee-rh'eem)

This is a fragrant oil used in almost every flavoring as a base. It can be compared to olive oil in European and Mediterranean cooking. My mother was always very conscious of the fat and oil content of food. She assured me of the lightness and the healthiness of sesame oil. The oil is available in most American markets. Take care to read the ingredients label as sometimes sesame oils are mixtures of sesame and vegetable oils. It is better to look around in Oriental markets for pure sesame oil.

Sesame Seeds and Sesame Salt
(que-soogim)

Sesame, recognizable by its nutty aroma, is used in a lot of Asian dishes. Koreans use it as a seasoning as well as a garnish on foods. When it is a garnish, the sesame seeds are used whole, and as a seasoning it is used in a saltlike consistency to blend in better with the sauce. Korean markets offer large packages of whole sesame seeds and sesame seeds already toasted and ground into a "salt."

My mother used to toast sesame seeds to make her own sesame salt. One of my fondest childhood memories was how I would hold my face over the mortar to get a whiff of this rich aroma as my mother ground the seeds.

To make your own sesame salt, generously cover the surface of a frying pan with whole sesame seeds. Stir the sesame seeds around as they toast over a medium flame and turn from a pale tan color to a deep nutty brown. As the seeds begin to pop in the pan, pour them into a wide, flat sieving basket and shake it back and forth to cool the seeds. Then pour the seeds into a mortar and grind them with a pestle. As you grind the seeds with a rhythmic pound, take a whiff of this rich aroma.

Soybean Paste (dwen-jang)

Soybean paste is sometimes known as miso paste. It is easily found in any Asian market. Soybean paste has been used in Korea historically, and it is one of the most important ingredients as a soup or stew base in Korean cuisine. My mother remembers when her family had little to eat after the Korean War. They savored bowls of soups that were made with soybean paste, cabbage, and bean sprouts.

Refried soybean paste also makes a hearty and pungent sauce. The same method and ingredients are used to make this sauce as the red pepper sauce listed on page 8. My mother prefers the soybean sauce for beef barbecues.

Sprouts (namul)

There are two popular sprouts in Korean cooking: the soybean sprout and mungbean sprout. An untrained eye can easily mistake one for the other. Familiarize yourself with both kinds since they are not always interchangeable. Soybean sprouts, called *kong-namul,* are long and feel crispy. The heads resemble yellow beans. The mungbean sprouts, called *sook-ju namul,* are much smaller and have heads that are budlike. Always look for fresh sprouts that are firm and unspeckled. Korean markets offer sprouts in large-quantity bags, since blanching, steaming, and boiling reduces them.

Tofu (*dubu*)

Tofu is one of the easiest ingredients to find in any market nowadays. Packaged tofu is good and will accommodate the recipes without a huge difference in taste. However, since tofu is commonly used in Asian cooking, fresh tofu in Oriental supermarkets is best. Tofu is usually fresh when the holding water is clear. If possible, try to smell the tofu. Any sour or pungent odor may indicate it is not fresh. After cooking, store remaining tofu in a bowl of clean, cold water. This will keep the tofu good only for a few days. For side dishes such as pan-fried or seasoned tofu, firm tofu is favored and is great in soups as well. Soft tofu is found already packaged in paper boxes located in the cooler section of the market.

Side Dishes
(Banchan)

반
찬

Banchan are best described in English as side dishes. Just as important as rice, a variety of banchan is served at every meal. At an elaborate, more formal Korean meal, there is no limit to how many banchan you will find. At home, we grew up eating a basic selection of side dishes: kimchi, seasoned bean sprouts, fresh chili peppers with soybean paste dips, pickled garlic, a chive or spinach salad.

Banchan can be prepared with any kind of food—vegetables, beef, seafood, fish. Here, we've selected banchan using only vegetables, since these recipes are my mother's favorites. My mother believes in a balanced meal, never overemphasizing one type of food such as beef, and always eating plenty of vegetables.

The array of banchan my mother prepares usually complements or counteracts the spiciness (or lack of spiciness) of the main dish. For instance, a spicy chicken dish would be served with a sesame-dressed spinach salad, and a mildly seasoned fish bake would be complemented by a cucumber salad seasoned with red pepper.

Despite tradition, most Korean cooks have their own way of preparing banchan. My mother makes hers using simple ingredients, seasoning lightly. She believes in bringing out the taste of the vegetables as much as possible.

The vegetables used to make banchan are raw, blanched, or slightly cooked. My mother prefers them crisp, preserving their natural texture and nutrients.

My favorite banchan is the pickled garlic. Mom would make it on weekends, filling mammoth-size jars with whole garlic cloves packed in soy sauce. When ready to eat, the garlic cloves are served cold. They're delicious. My mother would restrict me to only two or three pieces at a time because she was afraid I might reek of garlic!

When we think of Korean food, particularly banchan, we can't help but think of kimchi. Kimchi is best described as pickled cabbage. Using a potent combination of garlic, onions, and red pepper powder and flakes, the spiciness is tangy and mouth-watering. Almost every Korean meal needs to be complemented with kimchi as the "spicy agent." The ingredients are simple and a good batch of kimchi will last to make a hearty stew, appetizing pancakes, a refreshing mixture for noodles, and a good smothering rice stir-fry.

Seasoned Spinach

Shigim-chi moochim

1 POUND FRESH SPINACH
1 TEASPOON COARSE SALT

sauce:
1 TABLESPOON SOY SAUCE
1 TEASPOON SESAME OIL
1 TEASPOON SESAME SALT
1 TEASPOON CRUSHED GARLIC
½ TEASPOON MINCED SCALLION
1½ TEASPOONS RED PEPPER SAUCE (SEE PAGE 8)
1½ TEASPOONS VINEGAR
1 TEASPOON BROWN SUGAR

1. Prepare the spinach by cutting off the roots and separating the leaves.

2. In boiling water, dissolve 1 teaspoon of salt and blanch the spinach for no more than 1 minute. Turn the spinach over once in the boiling water and strain immediately. Rinse thoroughly with water. Keep aside.

3. In a mixing bowl, stir together all the ingredients for seasoning the spinach. Then add the spinach and toss with your hands in a massaging motion.

NOTE: To prepare spinach for bibimbop (see page 56), season the spinach mildly, omitting from the sauce the vinegar, sugar, and red pepper paste.

The mildly seasoned spinach will last longer refrigerated, without the acidity.

SERVES 2

시금치 무침

Seasoned Eggplant

Gagi moochim

A good side dish to accompany a barbecue beef or fish dish, the gagi moochim is really a free agent and appropriate at any meal. Very bountiful and healthy, the Korean version of an eggplant salad is delicate and mouthwatering. In any kitchen, with some simple seasonings and eggplants, it can be prepared in minutes. Served cold, the eggplant salad is perfect in the summer with rice, noodles, or as a delicious ingredient in a sandwich. Also tasty for vegetarians and for people who want to eat light, eggplants are fat-free.

2 MEDIUM CHINESE EGGPLANTS, APPROXIMATELY 8 OUNCES
  TOTAL, UNPEELED
1 TABLESPOON SOY SAUCE
1 TEASPOON CRUSHED GARLIC
1 TEASPOON MINCED SCALLION
½ TEASPOON RED PEPPER FLAKES (OPTIONAL)
1 TEASPOON VINEGAR
1 TEASPOON SESAME OIL
1 TEASPOON SESAME SALT

1. Halve the eggplants and steam for 15 minutes, until well cooked. Allow to sit in covered pot for 5 minutes.

2. Remove from pot and, using your hands, shred the eggplant coarsely.

3. In a mixing bowl, add all seasonings to the eggplant and mix together in a massaging motion using your hands. This salad will keep for 2 days.

SERVES 4

I have three daughters and a husband. The five of us make up our family. Twenty-four years ago, my husband and I got married. Although my husband did not have a formal education, he was always intuitive and creative. When he was younger, he was a very hardworking man. Back in Korea, he worked as a contractor and built four houses. He was not formally trained, but he relied on his vision and had a natural gift for it. Everyone thought so: he was known as the man that liked building things with his hands. He bought land and built these houses. He sold three of them. He kept the fourth house because it was very hard to sell at the time. It took my husband over a year to build it. The neighborhood where this house still stands has become very exclusive these days. Back then, this area was incredibly underdeveloped. Out of the four houses my husband built in Korea, the biggest and the most beautiful one, was the house we spent our lives in before we came here. My oldest daughter, Jenny, remembers this house.

This house was built at the foot of a mountain. It was three stories high. There was a yard in front where my husband built a stone garden. Flowers sprouted between the crevices of the stone. In the spring, these flowers were always the first to bloom in the neighborhood. To me there was nothing more beautiful than our garden.

Every day at noon, our peacocks would spread their wings. My husband and I loved these birds and tended to them daily. He also built a swimming pool. At the time no one had one; it was simply unimaginable. We relaxed by the pool with our children. When Jenny was four years old, I gave birth to Moon Sun, then a year later to Jane. And in this house was where I planned to raise our children.

Inside the house, my husband also built a water fountain. He constructed it using rocks and it was designed perfectly. When it rained, water would trickle down the fountain into our living room. I remember feeling overwhelmed when I first laid eyes on it. What my husband had envisioned for us was ingenious.

Later after the completion of the house, my husband was diagnosed with diabetes. He became physically weak. Eating healthily became an important part of our lives. I ventured into a little business of my own, a small restaurant. The restaurant was small but pretty exclusive. You couldn't eat there without reservations. Because I paid attention to the food as if I were feeding my family, the clientele was really appreciative. It was very rewarding when a customer would run into the kitchen to compliment me on the meal. It was hard work, but to see people so pleased was worth it.

Seasoned Perilla Leaves

Quen-neep

Seasoned perilla leaves are eaten over a scoop of rice. My mother particularly loves this banchan. She prepares quen-neep, stores it in pint-size containers, and snacks on it with rice during the summer when she wants to eat light. Quen-neep is favored for its minty, refreshing, and astringent quality. Steamed or seasoned, the perilla leaf is fibrous enough to keep up to 4 days.

1 BUNCH PERILLA LEAVES, WASHED AND STRAINED

sauce:
4 TABLESPOONS SOY SAUCE
1 TABLESPOON SESAME SALT
1 TABLESPOON FINELY MINCED SCALLION
2 TABLESPOONS FINELY MINCED ONION
1 TABLESPOON CRUSHED GARLIC
1 TABLESPOON RED PEPPER FLAKES
2 TABLESPOONS SESAME OIL
1 TEASPOON BROWN SUGAR

1. In a mixing bowl, combine all the ingredients for the sauce and mix together using a fork.

2. In a container or a deep bowl, spread some sauce on the bottom and spread individual sheets of perilla leaves on top of it. Apply the sauce to each perilla leaf and stack in the container or bowl. Refrigerate to keep for a few days.

The perilla leaves can be steamed, if you prefer, and served with the sauce.

SERVES 3 TO 4

My mother's recipe for a perfect batch of kimchi includes red pepper flakes, sea salt, napa cabbage, and cubes of radish. My grandmother, my mother, and I, in Korea around 1976.

Our childhood memories include end-less piano lessons and weekend outings with our friends from church, and Mom in the kitchen preparing side dishes (banchan) to last the week. Ingredients (counterclockwise): gwari (twist peppers), Chinese eggplants, sea-soned chrysanthemum leaves, toasted corn kernels to make tea, turnip, dried seaweed, seasoned soybean sprouts, giant white radish, and (center) toast-ed sesame for making sesame salt.

Moon Sun remembers a day when she went digging for fresh clams and Mom used them to make her favorite soup— Cho-gae tang—a soup of spinach and clams.

Homemade dumplings and rice cakes are important for making a soup eaten on special occasions, such as a first birthday, Harvest Day, or New Year's Day, to bring forth prosperity, good luck, and health.

A traditional afternoon snack: pumpkin porridge with a spinach salad, water kimchi, and a cup of hot ginger tea.

We often barbecued kalbi short ribs at the park and ate them with rice, bosam kimchi, and pan-fried tofu.

Table setting with Loosugui, which is served raw to grill at the table and eat right away, complemented by a scallion salad, sesame dip, cucumber salad, marinated soy beans, and seasoned radish. Remember to serve with fresh greens that can be used to make a "ssam"—a rice and beef wrap.

Spicy Chive Salad

Buchu moochim

8 OUNCES FRESH CHIVES
2 OUNCES GREEN CHILI PEPPER
2 TABLESPOONS SOY SAUCE
1 TEASPOON CRUSHED GARLIC
1 TEASPOON RED PEPPER FLAKES
1 TEASPOON SESAME SALT
1 TEASPOON BROWN SUGAR
1 TEASPOON SESAME OIL

1. Rinse the chives. Cut off up to an inch from the bulb and discard. Chop chives about 2 inches in length. Slice chili pepper into thin strips. Put aside.

2. In a mixing bowl, combine the soy sauce, garlic, red pepper flakes, sesame salt, brown sugar, and sesame oil with a spoon. Add in the chives and green chili pepper. Using your hands, gently but evenly mix in the seasoning. Serve immediately and eat before the chives wilt.

SERVES 3 TO 4

부추무침

Chrysanthemum Leaf Salad

Soogat moochim

METHOD 1

½ POUND CHRYSANTHEMUM LEAVES	1 TEASPOON RICE VINEGAR
1 TEASPOON SOY SAUCE	½ TEASPOON MINCED SCALLION
½ TEASPOON CRUSHED GARLIC	1 TEASPOON BROWN SUGAR
1 TEASPOON SESAME SALT	1 TEASPOON BLACK PEPPER

1. Clean chrysanthemum leaves and strain. Cut into coarse, and generous sizes.

2. In a mixing bowl, stir together the soy sauce, garlic, sesame salt, vinegar, minced scallion, sugar, and black pepper. Add chrysanthemum leaf and toss gently, using your hand. Serve immediately.

METHOD 2

1 POUND CHRYSANTHEMUM LEAVES
1 TEASPOON COARSE SALT

dipping sauce:	
4 TABLESPOONS RED PEPPER PASTE	1 TEASPOON SOY SAUCE
1 TABLESPOON WATER	1 TEASPOON CRUSHED GARLIC
1 TABLESPOON RICE VINEGAR	1 TABLESPOON BROWN SUGAR
	½ TEASPOON MINCED SCALLION
	½ TEASPOON SESAME SALT

1. Clean chrysanthemum leaves and strain. This time, use them whole. In boiling hot water, dissolve 1 teaspoon of salt and blanch the leaves for not more than a minute. Strain.

2. With each leaf, make a loop and wind it up holding on to one end. Tuck in to prevent it from undoing.

3. In a bowl, combine the dipping sauce ingredients.

4. Take the chrysanthemum leaf knots and make a neat arrangement on a plate and serve chilled with the dipping sauce on the side.

SERVES 2 TO 3

쑥갓무침

Seasoned Radish

Moosang-che

1¼ POUNDS WHITE RADISH, CHOPPED VERY FINE OR SHREDDED
WITH A FOOD SLICER (SEE ILLUSTRATION BELOW)
1 TABLESPOON COARSE SALT
1½ TABLESPOONS VINEGAR
2 TABLESPOONS SUGAR
1½ TABLESPOONS RED PEPPER POWDER
1 TEASPOON CRUSHED GARLIC

1. In a mixing bowl, combine all the ingredients using your hand.
Then strain the liquid from the seasoned radish before serving or storing.
Too much liquid dilutes the spicy flavor of seasoned radish. Serve chilled
for maximum flavor.

SERVES 2 TO 3

무우생채

Spicy Cucumber Salad

Oye moochim

1½ POUNDS KIRBY OR KOREAN CUCUMBERS
2 TABLESPOONS COARSE SALT
1½ TABLESPOONS RED PEPPER FLAKES
1 TABLESPOON RICE VINEGAR
1 TEASPOON SESAME SALT
1 TEASPOON CRUSHED GARLIC
1 TEASPOON SESAME OIL
1 TABLESPOON BROWN SUGAR

1. Slice cucumber into thin rounds. Use a food slicer to make it easier. In a mixing bowl, evenly sprinkle the coarse salt on the cucumber. Allow it to sit for 20 minutes. The salt not only helps to season the cucumber, but also to absorb the water from the cucumber.

2. Strain the cucumber. There are two easy ways to do this thoroughly. One way is to wring the water out using a piece of cheesecloth. The other way is to use a wire strainer, putting a heavy object on the cucumber to press out excess water. After the cucumber has been strained, keep it aside in a mixing bowl.

3. In a separate bowl, stir together the red pepper flakes, rice vinegar, sesame salt, garlic, sesame oil, and sugar. Then combine the dressing with the cucumber and toss, using your hands to mix in the seasonings evenly. Serve it whenever you like, but keep it chilled. The taste is more refreshing this way.

SERVES 2 TO 3

오이무침

Seasoned Soybean Sprouts

Kong-namul

When my mother prepared seasoned soybean sprouts, the head of the bean sprout was the one part I wouldn't eat. I preferred to eat only the stem. The heads sat in my bowl, which would have been empty had I not been so fussy about the bean heads.

1 POUND FRESH SOYBEAN SPROUTS (SEE PAGE 12-13)
½ CUP WATER
2 TABLESPOONS VEGETABLE OIL
1 TEASPOON CRUSHED GARLIC
1 TEASPOON SALT
1 TEASPOON SESAME SALT
1 TEASPOON MINCED SCALLION

1. Wash the soybean sprouts and remove the shell of the soybean sprout heads using water. Strain. Put aside.

2. In a mixing bowl, stir together the water, vegetable oil, garlic, and salt to make the sauce.

3. In a pot, combine the bean sprouts with the sauce on top. Cover and cook for 7 minutes over a medium flame. Turn off the fire, but keep the lid on and let it sit for 5 minutes.

4. Remove lid and turn over the bean sprouts once, Add the sesame salt and minced scallion and it is ready to serve. Tasty hot or chilled.

SERVES 3 TO 4

"It is the most nutritious part," my mother would say.
"Well, then I'll just drink more milk," I said.
"It will make you prettier."
"Nope. You said that about the green onions."
Now, after eighteen years, I eat them whole.
— Jane Kwak

호박볶음

Zucchini Sauté

Hobak bokum

4 MEDIUM-SIZE ZUCCHINI
2 TABLESPOONS SALAD OIL
1 TEASPOON COARSE SALT
1 TEASPOON CRUSHED GARLIC
1 TEASPOON SESAME SALT

1. Clean zucchini thoroughly. Halve the zucchini and slice into thin semi-circles. Use a shredder to make it even easier.

2. In a pan suitable to sauté, mix together the zucchini with salad oil, salt, and garlic and sauté for 5 minutes over a high flame. Sauté for 2 more minutes over a medium flame. Sprinkle with sesame salt.

3. Immediately remove to a plate to prevent the zucchini from getting soggy. Serve hot or cold; it's tasty both ways.

SERVES 3 TO 4

Gobo Turnip Sauté

Wu-ung bokum

Gobo turnips are two to three feet long and brown in color with a hairy texture. You can find these turnips in Asian markets.

1 POUND GOBO TURNIPS
3 TABLESPOONS SOY SAUCE
1 TABLESPOON BROWN SUGAR
2 TABLESPOONS VEGETABLE OIL
¼ CUP WATER
1 TEASPOON SESAME SEEDS

1. Shave the turnip using a carrot peeler. Cut into slender strips about 1 inch long. Cook in boiling water. Bite into a piece to test if the turnip is done; it should be chewable. Strain and keep aside.

2. In a mixing bowl, combine the soy sauce, brown sugar, vegetable oil, and water.

3. In a cooking pot, mix the sauce in with the gobo turnip. Without using a lid, cook over a medium flame until the liquid evaporates and the turnip seems to have absorbed most of the sauce.

4. Sprinkle on sesame seeds. Tasty served cold or hot, and will keep for up to a week refrigerated.

SERVES 3 TO 4

우엉볶음

Potato Sauté

Gamja bokum

3 IDAHO POTATOES, PEELED AND CLEANED
1 GREEN CHILI PEPPER (SEE PAGE 6)
2 TABLESPOONS VEGETABLE OIL
½ TEASPOON COARSE SALT
1 TEASPOON CRUSHED GARLIC
1 TEASPOON SESAME SALT
PINCH OF BLACK PEPPER

1. Chop the potatoes into julienne, keeping the strips thin. Soak in water for 7 to 10 minutes. Strain the potato and use a paper towel to pat the potato dry. Halve the chili pepper, remove seeds, and slice the pepper into thin strips.

2. In a frying pan, sauté the potato with oil, salt, and garlic for 7 to 10 minutes over a medium flame. The potato should be cooked, but not so soft that it crumbles. Add the sesame salt and black pepper and sauté for about a minute. Ready to serve.

SERVES 2 TO 3

감자 볶음

Sautéed Seaweed

Miyuk bokum

1 GENEROUS HANDFUL OF DRIED SEAWEED PIECES, SOAKED IN
   WATER FOR ABOUT 10 MINUTES, WASHED AND STRAINED
1½ TABLESPOONS SALAD OIL
5 GARLIC CLOVES, THINLY SLICED
1 TEASPOON SESAME SALT
¼ TEASPOON COARSE SALT

Mix together all the ingredients in a pan. Cover and cook over a medium flame for about 7 minutes. Remove lid and sauté for 5 minutes over a medium flame. Ready to serve.

SERVES 2 TO 3

Dried Anchovy Sauté

Meddruchi bokum

1½ CUPS DRIED ANCHOVIES, TINY ONES ABOUT 1 INCH LONG
6 TABLESPOONS SOY SAUCE
2 TEASPOONS CRUSHED GARLIC
2 TEASPOONS MINCED SCALLION
2 TABLESPOONS BROWN SUGAR
2 TABLESPOONS VEGETABLE OIL
23 TO 25 PIECES OF KOREAN TWIST PEPPERS, ABOUT 4 OUNCES
   (SEE PAGE 7)
1 TEASPOON SESAME SEEDS

1. In a frying pan or skillet over a medium flame, sauté the anchovies, 4 tablespoons of soy sauce, the garlic, scallion, sugar, and oil for 15 minutes, stirring. Keep aside.

2. Poke a hole through each pepper so that sauce can seep through while it is cooking.

3. In another frying pan, sauté the peppers for 5 minutes over a medium flame using 2 tablespoons of soy sauce. Remove from heat and combine the peppers with the anchovies and sauté together for 5 minutes over a medium flame. Sprinkle with sesame seeds. Serve hot or cold.

SERVES 5 TO 6

멸
치
볶
음

Omelet Roll

Geyran buchim

5 EGGS (FOR 2 ROLLS)
¼ TEASPOON COARSE SALT
2 TABLESPOONS MINCED SCALLION
7 TABLESPOONS VEGETABLE OIL

1. Beat eggs with salt and add minced scallion.
2. Heat oil in a large frying pan. Spread a thin layer of the egg batter and cook. As it cooks, use a spatula under an end, then fold over and over to make a roll as the egg cooks. Once in a roll, turn over to lightly brown the egg. Remove from heat and let the omelet roll cool.
3. Cut into slender pieces and serve it as a side dish with rice.

SERVES 3 TO 4

계란부침

Egg and Scallion Custard

Geyran jjim

4 EGGS
3 TABLESPOONS WATER
½ TEASPOON COARSE SALT
1 TABLESPOON MINCED SCALLION
1 TABLESPOON SESAME SALT
PINCH OF RED PEPPER POWDER
½ TABLESPOON SESAME OIL

1. In a metal bowl, or any heatproof bowl that will fit comfortably in a pot, beat the eggs with water and salt using a fork. Add the scallion, sesame salt, red pepper powder, and sesame oil and beat together.

2. Pour enough water into the pot so the bowl floats, with one third of the bowl under water. Cover and cook over a medium flame for 20 minutes. Add more water if it evaporates before the egg is done. Check to see if the egg is done by poking into it with a fork (if fork comes out clean, it is done).

3. Serve the egg custard in the bowl that it was steamed in and enjoy it while it is hot.

SERVES 3 TO 4

계
란
찜

Marinated Soybeans

Koing-jang

Soybeans are versatile and throughout time have been used efficiently, from fermenting soybeans for paste added to soups and sauces, as a base to make tofu or oil to nowadays making "fake" meat for vegetarians. Soybeans are pretty remarkable, and this recipe is another way to enjoy them. The beans are cooked semi-hard and have a nuttier quality than the well-cooked or steamed bean. Not meant to be gulped down in large quantities but merely sampled lightly, koing-jang complements most dishes quite well. Especially good with spicy soup, these soybeans have a touch of sweetness.

2 CUPS OF SOYBEANS (LOOK FOR ONES WITH THE BLACK PEEL)
2 TEASPOONS GARLIC JUICE
½ CUP SOY SAUCE
5 TABLESPOONS SALAD OIL
4 TABLESPOONS BROWN SUGAR

1. Cook the soybeans with 1 cup of water over a medium flame for 20 minutes, uncovered. Halfway through, spoon the top portion of the soybeans to the bottom, and the bottom to the top, so that the beans cook evenly. Remove pot after 20 minutes of cooking; the beans should feel semi-hard.

2. Keeping the soybeans in the pot, add the garlic, soy sauce, salad oil, and sugar and mix in using a spoon. Cook for 15 minutes more over a medium flame, stirring occasionally, until most of the liquid has evaporated.

3. Serve once the beans have cooled.

SERVES 5 TO 6

콩
장

Seasoned Bean Curd (Tofu)

Dubu buchim

METHOD 1
1¼ TO 1½ POUNDS FIRM TOFU
¼ CUP VEGETABLE OIL

sauce:
4 TABLESPOONS SOY SAUCE
1 TABLESPOON MINCED SCALLION
1 TABLESPOON RED PEPPER FLAKES
1 TABLESPOON SESAME SALT
1 TABLESPOON CRUSHED GARLIC
1 TABLESPOON SESAME OIL
1 TEASPOON BROWN SUGAR

1. Cut the tofu over a sheet of paper towel to absorb the water. Gently press down on the tofu with your free hand as you cut. Halve the tofu horizontally and cut into three sections vertically. Then make two cuts through sideways, leaving ¼-inch thickness.

2. Over a medium flame, heat a tablespoon or so of vegetable oil in a frying pan. Arrange the tofu in the frying pan without any overlapping and flip over once or twice. Try to handle tofu so that it does not crumble and avoid stirring it around in the pan. Cook the tofu until it browns. Continue with more oil until all the tofu is cooked.

3. Stir together all the sauce ingredients.

4. Serve on a plate in a neat arrangement and smear on the sauce before it goes to the table.

METHOD 2
The tofu can also be steamed or boiled and served with the sauce. It is very flavorful and ideal for those who want to stay away from fried foods.

SERVES 3 TO 4

두부부침

METHOD 3

Cut the tofu as in method 1, except cut only once through the side for thicker pieces of tofu.

sauce:

4 TABLESPOONS SOY SAUCE

3 TABLESPOONS SALAD OIL

2 TABLESPOONS RED PEPPER SAUCE (SEE PAGE 8)

1 TABLESPOON CRUSHED GARLIC

1 TABLESPOON MINCED SCALLION

1 TABLESPOON SESAME SALT

2 TABLESPOONS BROWN SUGAR

Mix all the ingredients with 2 tablespoons of water to make sauce. In a heavy pan, spread the sauce over the tofu. Cover and cook for 7 to 10 minutes over a medium flame. Cook until the sauce condenses. Serve while hot.

Napa Cabbage Kimchi, VERSION 1

Baechu-poghi kimchi

Kimchi is best described as pickled preserves that provide the spicy, sharp, and salty flavor in a meal. Kimchi is served at all meals of the day, all year round. It is also enjoyed with rice alone as a quick meal. Since kimchi is a main staple in Korean food, it is prepared using many types of vegetables, but the napa cabbage, otherwise known as Chinese cabbage, is the most traditional and popular.

There is a different type of kimchi appropriate for almost every season. Some vegetables are fresher than others in certain seasons, and the fresher the vegetable, the tastier the kimchi. During the summer, my mother prepared cucumber kimchi, which was always refreshing and enticing with fish, meat, or soup. Another one of our favorites was water kimchi, which always complemented beef-barbecue dishes. During the winter, we savored radish kimchi with our bowls of milky bone marrow soup and hot rice. One of my fondest memories of growing up was how on New Year's Day my mother served a newly made batch of kimchi with her homemade dumpling and rice cake soup. Cabbage kimchi will keep up to ten days. Leftover kimchi can be added to soup and stirfries. The longer kimchi has been aged, the tastier the dish.

2 NAPA CABBAGES (ABOUT 8 POUNDS)

1¼ CUPS COARSE SALT

5 TO 6 OUNCES GIANT WHITE RADISH

5 TABLESPOONS COARSE SALT

3 TABLESPOONS SUGAR

2 CUPS RED PEPPER FLAKES

2 TEASPOONS FINELY MINCED GINGERROOT

2 CUPS ONION JUICE

5 TABLESPOONS CRUSHED GARLIC

1. Quarter the cabbages lengthwise. Dissolve 1¼ cups of salt in 4 cups of water in a wide and shallow basin or bowl. Hold each stalk of the cabbage and rinse it thoroughly with the salt water, applying it between the leaves as well. Do not shake out all the salt water.

2. Place the soaked cabbage in a gallon-size container with large, clean stones on top of the cabbage to act as weights. Discard the remaining

배추포기김치

salt water. Cover the container and let the cabbage pickle for 4 hours with weights in place. Turn over and pickle for 4 more hours.

3. Shred the radish and combine it with the seasonings in a large mixing bowl. Mix together using your hands. Wearing a plastic glove, generously smear the seasoning on the cabbage stalks and fill in plentifully between the leaves as well. Pack the kimchi tightly in the gallon container. Cover the surface with plastic wrap, pressing down to get rid of all air pockets. Cover the jar. Store at 70 degrees for 48 hours to ferment.

4. Before serving, chop up kimchi stalks, carefully preserving the neat piles. Chill before eating.

Serves 5 to 6

Women prepared kimchi to last the whole winter in Korea. It was preserved by burying it in ceramic barrels beneath the ground to keep it from getting frozen or spoiled by the cold weather. Women pickled 2 to 3 ceramic barrels of kimchi at a time, and each ceramic barrel held 30 to 40 pounds of kimchi. The men helped their wives by digging up the ground deep enough to fit the ceramic barrels. Women had access to the kimchi by lifting the lid on the ceramic barrel throughout the cold months. Its strong, distinctive flavor was a familiar comfort all winter long.

HOW A CLEVER GRANDMOTHER USED
RED PEPPER POWDER TO
WARD OFF A GREEDY TIGER

The use of red pepper powder, the most important spice used in making kimchi, has prevailed for centuries. There is a Korean folktale about a grandmother, her clever tricks, a bad tiger, and the prized use of red pepper powder. It is a fable we were told in Korean school.

A little old grandmother, upon returning to her hut from the forest, was stopped by a hungry and mean tiger. He was about to eat her when the grandmother said, "No, don't eat me. I am not even appetizing. Come over to my hut tonight and I will make a delicious dinner for you to eat." Easily convinced, the tiger allowed her to pass. When nightfall came, the tiger went to her hut. The grandmother was calm and prepared for the tiger's visit.

During the day, she set up a series of traps to punish the bad tiger. One particular trap was a pot of water filled with red pepper powder that she was going to use to make kimchi.

When the tiger arrived, the grandmother invited him in, but politely asked the tiger to bring the brazier that was set just outside the room to keep her warm on cold nights. The tiger went to fetch the brazier for the old grandmother and saw that the fire was all burned out. The grandmother called, "If you blow really hard you can revive the fire." The tiger blew at the coals as hard as he could. All the ashes in the brazier blew into the air and into the tigers' eyes. "Oh, grandmother, I have ashes in my eyes, I cannot see!" the tiger cried.

The grandmother, still in her room, innocently told the howling tiger to wash his eyes out with the water in the pot beside him. So the tiger dunked his face in the pot of water to clean out his eyes. But little did he know that there was red pepper powder in the water. Now in even greater pain he cried for help.

Then the grandmother told him to wipe his eyes using the towel that lay next to the pot of water. The tiger did as told, not knowing that there were needles pricked into the towel. He yelped in pain and, convinced that the grandmother had called some goblins to get him, he ran away to escape them. Blinded, he ran off a cliff, plunging to his death. That was the last of the bad tiger, and the end of a story about a grandmother and her clever tricks.

Napa Cabbage Kimchi, VERSION 2

Baechu mock kimchi

4 POUNDS NAPA CABBAGE
¾ CUP COARSE SALT

seasonings:
1 TEASPOON FINELY MINCED GINGERROOT
1 CUP RED PEPPER POWDER
2 TABLESPOONS SUGAR
3 TABLESPOONS GARLIC JUICE
1 CUP ONION JUICE
4 OUNCES SCALLIONS, CUT INTO 1-INCH LENGTHS
3 TABLESPOONS COARSE SALT

1. Coarsely chop the cabbage into 1-inch pieces. Place in a container. Dissolve ¾ cup of salt in 2 cups of water and pour over the cabbage. Use your hand to mix it in evenly. Cover and let it pickle for 3 hours. Toss and turn over and pickle it for 3 more hours. Strain the cabbage and discard the salt water.

2. In a mixing bowl, combine all the seasonings and mix. Add the scallion last. Let it sit for 10 minutes. Distribute the seasoning on the cabbage and blend in using your hands.

3. Tightly pack the cabbage in a gallon-size jar. Cover the surface with plastic wrap and press down to get rid of air pockets. Store at 70 degrees for 24 hours to ferment. Chill before serving.

SERVES 5 TO 6

배추막김치

Cucumber Kimchi

Oye kimchi

2 POUNDS KIRBY OR KOREAN CUCUMBERS, UNPEELED
½ CUP COARSE SALT

seasonings:
4 OUNCES SCALLIONS, FINELY MINCED
4 OUNCES FRESH CHIVES, CUT INTO ½-INCH LENGTHS
2 TABLESPOONS CRUSHED GARLIC
3 TABLESPOONS RED PEPPER FLAKES
1 TABLESPOON COARSE SALT

1. Scrub the cucumbers and chop off the ends. Cut three grooves into the cucumbers lengthwise, carefully plunging the knife about halfway in. Place the cucumbers in a container. Dissolve ½ cup of coarse salt in ½ cup of water and pour over the cucumbers. Cover and pickle for 3 hours. Toss and turn over. Pickle for 3 more hours. By now, the cucumber should feel flimsy and flexible. Discard the water and put the cucumber aside.

2. In a mixing bowl, combine the seasonings except the salt and use your hand to mix it evenly. Being careful not to overstuff, place a generous amount of seasoning into the grooves in the cucumbers. Pack the cucumbers in a gallon-size container as you go along.

3. Pour 3 cups of water into the mixing bowl with leftover seasonings and rinse it out into a cooking pot. Bring it to a quick boil of about 100 degrees and allow it to cool at room temperature until it is 60 degrees.

4. Dissolve 1 tablespoon of coarse salt in the cooled water and pour over the cucumbers. Cover the surface with plastic wrap, pressing down to keep any air pockets from forming. Cover the container with a lid. Store at 70 degrees for 30 to 35 hours to ferment. Chill before serving.

SERVES 5 TO 6

오
이

김
치

Cubed Radish Kimchi

Gakdoo-ghee

4 POUNDS GIANT WHITE RADISH
½ CUP COARSE SALT

seasonings:
1 CUP RED PEPPER FLAKES
4 TABLESPOONS GARLIC JUICE
½ CUP ONION JUICE
2 TABLESPOONS COARSE SALT
2 TEASPOONS GINGERROOT JUICE
2 TABLESPOONS BROWN SUGAR

1. Wash the radish thoroughly and cut into ½-inch cubes. Store in a gallon container and evenly sprinkle on the ½ cup of coarse salt. Toss with your hand to smear the salt over the radish. Cover and let it pickle for 2 hours. Toss, using your hands, and pickle for another 2 hours. By now, some water should be collected on the bottom. Discard the salt water.

2. In a large mixing bowl, combine all the seasonings and mix together. Apply the seasoning to the radish and blend in evenly using your hand. Tightly pack the kimchi in a gallon jar. The less air, the better. Cover the surface with plastic wrap, pressing down to get rid of any air pockets. Cover the jar with a lid. Store at 70 degrees for 24 hours to ferment. Chill before serving.

SERVES 10 TO 12

깍뚜기

Bachelor Radish Kimchi

Chong-gac kimchi

The term "bachelor" is used to describe this kind of radish because its roughage, or leafy parts, are wild, plentiful, and untamed like a bachelor before he gets married.

4 POUNDS YOUNG RADISH
¾ CUP COARSE SALT

seasonings:
1 CUP RED PEPPER POWDER
3 TABLESPOONS COARSE SALT
2 TABLESPOONS SUGAR
4 TABLESPOONS GARLIC JUICE
½ CUP ONION JUICE
2 TEASPOONS GINGERROOT JUICE

1. Clean the radish thoroughly. Quarter it, and coarsely chop the greens. Store it in a gallon jar or plastic container. Put aside.

2. Dissolve ¾ cup of coarse salt in 1 cup of water. Evenly distribute the salt water on the radish and toss around using your hand. Cover and let it pickle for 3 hours. Toss and turn over to distribute the salt water evenly. Cover and let it pickle for 7 to 8 hours. Discard the salt water and rinse the radish and greens thoroughly with water. Keep aside in a basin or a container large enough to mix in the seasonings.

3. In a mixing bowl, combine the seasonings and use your hands to mix it evenly. Then apply the seasoning to the radish and greens. Blend in the seasoning thoroughly using your hands.

4. Pack the radish and greens tightly back into the gallon jar or container. Cover the surface of kimchi with plastic wrap, making sure all areas are covered. Press down to avoid any air pockets. Any slight exposure to air will bruise the surfacing kimchi. Cover the jar and store at 70 degrees for 48 hours to ferment. Refrigerate to keep up to 2 weeks. Use in soup when it turns sour (see page 69).

SERVES 10 TO 12

Water Kimchi

Dongchi-me

6 POUNDS GIANT WHITE RADISH, ABOUT 2 RADISHES
4 TABLESPOONS COARSE SALT

seasonings:
2 GARLIC CLOVES, THINLY SLICED
2 TABLESPOONS COARSE SALT
2 TABLESPOONS SUGAR
6 TO 7 THINLY SLICED PIECES OF GINGERROOT

1. Peel the radish and wash with water. Cut each radish into 6 to 8 pieces. Place it in a container and evenly sprinkle on 4 tablespoons of coarse salt. Pickle for 2 hours. Toss and turn over. Pickle for 3 more hours.

2. Separate the radish from the salt water that results and save the salt water. The salt water is used to make the broth in which this kimchi is served. After separating take the broth and using a fine mesh strainer filter out the particles that may be floating there. Combine the salt water, 5 cups of water, and the seasonings.

3. Pack the radish in a jar or container and pour in the seasoned water. Cover the surface with plastic wrap and press down to get rid of any air pockets. Cover the jar. Store at 70 degrees for 48 hours to ferment. Chill before serving. Cut up the radish in chunks and serve with water kimchi broth in a shallow bowl.

SERVES 15 TO 20

동
치
미

Pickled Garlic

Manil jang-ajji

1 POUND OF GARLIC, ABOUT 6 LARGE CLOVES
2½ CUPS SOY SAUCE
1 CUP RICE VINEGAR
½ CUP BROWN SUGAR

1. Slice the peeled garlic cloves into generous portions. Put it in a half-gallon-size jar (or any glass jar big enough to hold a pound of garlic). In a mixing bowl, stir the soy sauce, vinegar, and sugar together and it pour over the garlic in the jar. Spread plastic wrap over the top, covering the surface of garlic and liquid. Make sure there are no air pockets between the garlic and plastic. Exposure to any air will soften or bruise the surfacing garlic. Store at 60 to 70 degrees for 5 days, then refrigerate for 15 days.

2. On the twenty-first day, separate the garlic from the juice by pouring the juice carefully into another container, leaving the garlic in the jar. In a pot, boil the garlic juice to cleanse it of any impurities. Cool the liquid entirely at room temperature and pour it back into the jar with the garlic. Chill the jar of garlic until it is ready to be served. Serve in tiny portions.

NOTE: This method of pickling is easy and often done in homes. For the successful pickler, try this recipe with onions or peppers. For the onion, cut 1 pound of onion into strips and follow the same recipe. For pickling peppers, use a Korean pepper, called gwari, or twist pepper. It is mild, not spicy, and is about the size of a jalapeño pepper. Look for this pepper in Asian markets. Using 1 pound of peppers, follow the same recipe, except poke a hole through the peppers using a chopstick or a fork. The hole allows for the passage of the juice as it pickles.

SERVES 15 TO 20

마늘 장아찌

Rice and Noodle Dishes
(Bop)

밥과 국수

Rice is the food I value most. No matter how good and and well prepared a pot of soup, beef marinade, or spicy sauté of squid, a Korean dish is incomplete without a bowl of rice. Without it, I am lost—no past, present, or future. Rice keeps me alive, physically and spiritually. It is my comfort food, reminding me of home, who I am, and where I come from.

In a Korean meal, the bowl of rice is your base—everything you eat is piled on top. In the kitchen, rice was the first thing my mother set out to cook. Only afterward would she move on to make the fish, meat, and vegetables.

My favorite childhood recipe was Mom's fluffy egg custard, browned potato strips, and bite-size pieces of pan-fried tofu. With a scoop of hot rice straight out of the rice cooker, our breakfast was complete .

There was always rice in our home. I would sometimes invite a gang of friends over after school to feast on my mother's cooking. With the rice still warm in the cooker, I would heat up some stewed kalbi ribs, empty out the containers of my favorite seasoned vegetables from the refrigerator, and set up a feast on the table. Then my friends and I would eat madly to the last bite. Rice, since childhood, was the comfort food that brought it all together.

Once upon a time, there lived a blind man who had a daughter by the name of Shim Chong-yi. They were poor, and she had no mother, so Chong-yi worked hard to feed them. A countess offered to adopt the diligent girl. Chong-yi refused, as she would not leave the side of her blind father. The countess treated the young girl to a fancy dinner instead.

Night was falling and the father went to look for his daughter. On the way, he fell into a stream and a Buddhist monk ran to rescue him. The monk promised he could regain his eyesight if he offered the temple three hundred bags of rice and prayed. The blind man had no idea how to get the rice. When Chong-yi returned, he told her of his despair and she prayed to the Gods for help.

The next day sailors arrived looking for a young girl to sacrifice to the Sea God for the merchant ship's safe passage. Chong-yi offered herself in exchange for three hundred bags of rice. When the sailors came for her, she confessed to her unknowing father that she was to be sacrificed, and against his wishes she left with them for the seas. There, she prayed once more and dove into the angry ocean. The Heavens pitied Chong-yi for sacrificing her life for her father and told the Sea God to spare her, then she awoke in the Dragon palace with her mother. The Sea God then returned her as a beautiful lotus blossom that was brought to the king. It blossomed into Chong-yi and he made her his bride. Now a queen, she still grieved for her father. One day, after much searching, a poor blind man came to the palace. It was her father! He tried to look at her in joy as they embraced. It was a miracle! He could see again! In the presence of his daughter, his eyesight was restored.

Red Beans and Rice

Paht bop

While this might sound like the Mexican dish, it is actually a variation on a Korean staple—white rice.

My mother preferred to steam rice with red beans during the winter. This way, the rice was more substantial, supplying us with extra nutrients. It gave us stamina and kept us healthy during the months when we were prone to flu.

½ CUP SMALL RED BEANS
2 CUPS WHITE RICE

1. Soak the red beans for at least 24 hours. Reserve the water after straining the beans.

2. Combine the rice and beans in a heavy pot and measure in 3½ cups of water using the reserved water. If short, add water. Cook for 15 minutes over a medium flame. Set the lid ajar to allow the water to evaporate and cook for 5 minutes. Then cover the pot and simmer for 15 minutes. Serve hot.

SERVES 3 TO 4

Barley and Rice

Bori bop

Besides being a hearty, delicious dish, this recipe yields an extra surprise. The crust formation around the pot was used to make a tasty tea to drink after dinner. My mother would toast the rice stuck on the pot by heating the remains on the stove for a few minutes. Then she'd add some water and let it boil. She would drink this hot barley-flavored water to help settle her stomach after a good meal. And for her there was nothing more soothing—you could tell by the way she sighed after a few sips.

1½ CUPS BARLEY
¾ CUP WHITE RICE

1. Soak the barley in water for 24 hours.
2. In a heavy pot, combine 3 cups of water with the drained barley and rice. Cover and cook for 15 minutes over a medium flame. Uncover and cook for 5 minutes. Cover the pot once again and simmer for 25 minutes over a low flame. Serve hot.

SERVES 2 TO 3

MY GRANDMOTHER'S KOREAN KITCHEN

Before rice cookers, gas stoves, and hot water heaters, my mother's memory of the kitchen was collecting fallen twigs, branches, and leaves to burn for fire since the government prohibited the cutting of trees. The fire was lit on the ground inside a clay receptacle with three or four cavities on the top that held the cast-iron pots in place. The pots were suspended over the top to hold their weight. The fire that was used to cook was also used to heat the bedrooms because the rooms were built on a platform elevated from the ground. And because of the construction of the house, the heat from the fire in the kitchen would travel beneath the rooms, keeping them warm during the winter. A room heated in this way is called andel-bah'ng. *To this day, my mother prefers this source of heat.*

When my mother was a girl, a Korean house was not an American's idea of a typical house. The perimeter of the house was enclosed with brick walls, and a gate served as the entrance to the house. In the backyard, there was a vegetable and herb garden. Sometimes, there was a well for water. The main room, which was located in the center of the house, was lined with doors that slid open on parallel sides of the room. This created an "open" room, allowing cool breezes to pass through during the summer. This is where the family gathered to eat dinner, which was served on a low table. Families would sit on the floor of the platform room, shoes removed.

As a little girl, my mother would tend to the fire, feeding it wood, while her mother would tend to the cooking. The first pot held hot water to drink and cook with and to do dishes with after dinner, the second pot was used to cook rice, and the third pot stored the soup. The methods of cooking revolved around conserving the heat. Vegetables or eggs would be cooked last because these foods needed less heat. My mother remembers how her mother would place bean sprouts on the rice while the rice was steaming and in the end the sprouts would be cooked just right. And as her mother prepared dinner, my mother would help by setting the table, just as I was taught to help my mother. While the surroundings have changed, many of the traditions live on.

Rice with a Variety of Grains

Jaht-goke bop

Sixty to seventy years ago, native Koreans steamed rice with a variety of grains and beans for added nutritional value. This rice recipe is associated with pride and tradition for many Koreans. It's comfort food that warms and heals.

This rice is traditionally prepared in huge portions. Save and reheat by steaming the rice.

½ CUP BLACK BEANS
½ CUP SMALL RED BEANS
1 CUP BARLEY
1 CUP BROWN RICE
1 CUP SWEET RICE

1. Soak the black beans, red beans, barley, and brown rice for at least 24 hours. Reserve the water in which the black beans and red beans were soaking to use as a natural colorant when cooking the rice.

2. In a heavy pot, combine all the grains and beans. Measure in 3 cups water using the reserved water, adding fresh water if it falls short. Cover and cook over a medium flame for 15 minutes. Rest the lid slightly ajar to allow some water to evaporate and cook for 15 minutes. Then cover and simmer over a low flame for 20 to 30 minutes. Serve hot.

SERVES 7 TO 10

잡
곡
밥

Pumpkin Porridge

Hobac-juk

1 POUND YELLOW AND RIPE PUMPKIN, PREFERABLY KOBOCHA
   PUMPKIN
½ CUP RAW RICE, MIXED IN A BLENDER UNTIL COARSELY
   CRUSHED
4 OUNCES RICE CAKE
1 TEASPOON SALT
1 TABLESPOON BROWN SUGAR

garnish:
¼ CUP BLACK BEANS

1. Prepare black bean garnish: Boil beans in water for 5 minutes, then strain and set aside.

2. Peel the pumpkin, remove seeds, and chop into fine pieces. Using a heavy pot, cook the pumpkin with 12 cups of water for 30 minutes over a medium flame, covered. Stirring occasionally and watching to keep it from overflowing, partially lean the lid up. The pumpkin should be cooked to a purée; however, some clumps are good in this porridge.

3. Add the coarsely crushed rice with 1 cup of water to the purée and cook over a low flame for 20 minutes. Stir frequently to prevent the rice from burning on the bottom. Drop in cut up pieces of the rice cake, stir in the salt and sugar, and simmer for 5 more minutes. Garnish by mixing in some of the prepared black beans.

SERVES 3 TO 4

호
박
죽

Pine Nut Porridge

Jaht-jook

During the early mornings when my father rose at three to go to the fish market, he helped himself to breakfast while the family slept. He heated up a zippered bag of frozen pine nut porridge in boiling water and poured it into a shallow bowl. With ease, he prepared a hearty and warm breakfast to eat before driving out to the market.

¼ CUP BROWN RICE
¼ CUP WHITE RICE
1 CUP PINE NUTS
5 CUPS WATER
SALT TO TASTE

1. Soak the brown and white rice in water for at least 5 hours before preparing this dish. In a blender, combine ½ cup water with the drained rice and mix to get coarse but even bits of the rice. Put the rice in a heavy pot and keep aside.

2. Without rinsing out the residue of rice in the blender, combine ½ cup of water and the pine nuts, and mix to get coarse but even bits of the pine nuts. Add to the pot with the rice.

3. Pour 5 cups of water into the blender, rinse out the remaining residue, and pour it into the pot to cook the porridge. Stir constantly and cook over a medium flame for 20 minutes. If the soup is too thick, add a little water. But keep in mind that the porridge should not be watery. Cook for 7 more minutes over a low flame and stir constantly. By now the rice should be cooked and the porridge should be rich. Use salt to taste and serve while hot.

4. Save leftover porridge in zippered plastic bags in one-person portions and freeze. Reheat the bag in boiling water to enjoy this nutritious porridge another day.

SERVES 3 TO 4

잣
죽

Soybean Porridge

Beejee

This dish is one way Koreans savor the soybean. It requires special preparation, but it is well worth the effort. Soybean porridge is very filling on its own, and can be complemented with a side dish of some ripe kimchi, which is how my mother enjoys it, and how I like it too.

Refrigerated portions can be kept up to five days. Substitute beef or chicken for the pork, but keep in mind that most of the intensity of this dish comes from the soybean mash.

1½ CUPS WHITE-SHELL SOYBEANS, SOAKED IN WATER FOR
    24 HOURS
4 OUNCES LEAN PORK
½ TEASPOON BLACK PEPPER
1 TABLESPOON RICE WINE
½ TEASPOON SALT
½ TEASPOON SESAME OIL
1 POUND KIMCHI, PREFERABLY AGED AND SOUR, CUT INTO
    COARSE PIECES
1 TABLESPOON CRUSHED GARLIC
2 TABLESPOONS VEGETABLE OIL
½ CUP WATER

side sauce:
1 TEASPOON MINCED SCALLION
1 TEASPOON SESAME SALT
4 TABLESPOONS SOY SAUCE
1 TEASPOON RED PEPPER POWDER
2 TEASPOONS SESAME OIL
1 TEASPOON CRUSHED GARLIC
2 TABLESPOONS RICE VINEGAR
2 TABLESPOONS WATER

비
지

1. After 24 hours of soaking the soybeans in water, the shell should come apart easily, and most of the shell particles should rise to the surface of the water. Carefully pour away the shell particles floating on the surface

while using one hand to keep the soybeans from falling out of their container. Completely discarding the shells from the soybeans will make for a perfect soup. Continue to remove the shells by soaking in water again and plunging your hands into the water to rub off the shell. Pour away the surfacing particles and repeat this step until all the peel is discarded from the soybeans.

2. The soybeans should expand to 3 cups after being soaked. Use a blender to turn the soybeans into a thick, gruel-like consistency. Combine 1 cup of soybeans to 1 cup of water, and blend in short intervals. Repeat this three times. Set aside in a heavy pot.

3. Cut the pork into thin slices, and pound them using the blunt side of a knife. Season the pork with ½ teaspoon black pepper, 1 tablespoon of rice wine, ½ teaspoon coarse salt, and ½ teaspoon sesame oil. Combine the pork with kimchi, 1 tablespoon crushed garlic, and 2 tablespoons vegetable oil and sauté for 7 to 10 minutes over a medium-high flame. Keep aside.

4. Cook the soybean gruel by adding ½ cup of water and place over a medium-high flame while stirring constantly. When it boils and starts to overflow, reduce the flame. Cook for 15 minutes, stirring constantly. Add the sautéed pork and kimchi and cook for 10 to 15 minutes. Remove from heat.

5. Mix together the ingredients for the sauce. Serve it on the side with a saucer of soybean gruel. This dish will keep refrigerated for up to 5 days.

SERVES 3 TO 4

Rice and Vegetable Medley

Bibimbop

A classic Korean dish perfect for large gatherings, bibimbop is traditionally served buffet style. Each diner is served a mound of rice in a bowl, into which he or she mixes the vegetables, beef, and fish to taste, along with some of the red pepper sauce that makes the dish complete.

The vegetables used in bibimbop are similar to banchan (side dishes), including kimchi. For bibimbop, however, the vegetables are prepared with milder seasonings than usual, because of the red pepper sauce, which delivers quite a spicy kick.

Traditionally, bibimbop is a dish that is shared among women. When my mother was a young girl, food was scarce. Being resourceful and creative, the women of the household would feast on bibimbop made from a variety of leftovers, in deep clay bowls. Nowadays, bibimbop is served two different ways—in a heated clay bowl (called a tukbae-gee) or at room temperature during the summer. Either way, it's a healthy, filling, delicious meal. It's one of the most popular dishes at our restaurant—so popular that we decided to picture it on the cover of this book.

10 OUNCES LEAN BEEF (OPTIONAL)
2 MEDIUM ZUCCHINI
2 MEDIUM CUCUMBERS
4 OUNCES TURNIP OR DAIKON
4 OUNCES CARROTS
4 OUNCES SOYBEAN OR MUNG BEAN SPROUTS
4 OUNCES FRESH SPINACH
8 OUNCES CHEONG-PO (SEE PAGE 1) (OPTIONAL)
½ HEAD ROMAINE LETTUCE, COARSELY CHOPPED
4 EGGS

seasonings:

RED PEPPER FLAKES	SOY SAUCE
CRUSHED GARLIC	RICE VINEGAR
SESAME SALT	RICE WINE (SAKE)
SESAME OIL	BLACK PEPPER
VEGETABLE OIL	BROWN SUGAR

1. Prepare 4 servings of white rice.

2. To prepare the beef: Mince the beef and tenderize it by beating it with the dull side of a knife. Add 2 tablespoons soy sauce, 1 tablespoon rice wine, a pinch of crushed garlic, 1 teaspoon sesame oil, a pinch of black pepper, and 1 teaspoon of sugar. Using your hand, mix thoroughly. In a frying pan or skillet, cook until browned and set aside.

3. To season the vegetables: Scrub the zucchini and clean well. Halve the zucchini, then cut into thin slices. Using 1 teaspoon vegetable oil, a pinch of garlic, and a pinch of salt, sauté lightly over a low flame.

Clean and slice the cucumbers into thin pieces. Using a pinch of salt, a pinch of crushed garlic, and 1 teaspoon of rice vinegar, mix with your hands.

Clean and shred the turnip. Dress with the same seasonings used for the cucumber.

Clean and shred the carrots using a food slicer. In a saucepan with boiling water, blanch until semi-hard, about 2 minutes. Serve unseasoned.

Blanch the bean sprouts. Using a pinch of salt, a pinch of crushed garlic, 1 teaspoon of sesame oil, and a pinch of sesame salt, mix with your hand.

Season the spinach according to recipe and note on page 17.

Cut the cheong-po in strips and season with ½ teaspoon sesame oil and ½ teaspoon soy sauce.

4. To make the red pepper sauce: Using a wooden spoon, mix together 2 tablespoons red pepper paste, a pinch of crushed garlic, 1 teaspoon vinegar, 1 teaspoon water, and 1 teaspoon sesame oil.

5. In each of four medium bowls, place a small mound of rice, then make an even arrangement of the seasoned vegetables, beef, and romaine lettuce. Top off the bibimbop with a cooked or raw egg.

6. For hot bibimbop, place each clay bowl (tukbae-gee) directly on the flame of the stovetop burner until the bowl itself is hot.

7. Serve the red pepper sauce on the side and complement this dish with a side soup, preferably a mild one, and serve with kimchi. Eat the bibimbop with the contents all stirred up and add the red pepper sauce to your liking.

SERVES 4

Red Bean Porridge

Paht-juuk

2 CUPS SMALL RED BEANS
½ CUP RICE, WASHED AND SOAKED IN WATER FOR AT LEAST 20
    MINUTES
4 OUNCES RICE CAKE, THINLY SLICED

1. In a heavy pot, cook the red beans with 12 cups of water for 30 minutes over a medium flame. Stir frequently. Then cook for 40 more minutes over a low flame. Let the soup cool. The beans should look smothered and the consistency should be dense.

2. Remove the outer shells of the red beans. Use a mesh strainer and pour the bean soup through it. If the consistency is too thick, add some water to help separate the peel further and press the beans through the strainer.

3. Pour the strained soup back into the pot. Add the rice and 2 cups of water and cook for 15 minutes over a medium flame. Stir constantly. Over a low flame, cook for 15 minutes more, stirring. Add the rice cake and cook for 5 minutes, stirring. If the soup feels too thick, add a little water until it is the desired consistency.

SERVES 2 TO 3

Rice Cakes in Spicy Sauté

Dukboki

Like Thanksgiving in America, the Korean Harvest Day Festival is held in the chilly month of November. For this occasion, grown-ups and children alike dress in their traditional gowns. Cultural dances are performed onstage by children and professional dancers, and there is a very popular singing contest. The festival also bustles with food stalls that sell food native Koreans love, from soybean hot cakes, to blood sausages, to rice cakes cooked in a spicy sauce. Our parents always watched the show as my sisters and I wandered around to check out the food stalls. Our favorite was dukboki. I remember running back to find our parents to get some more money to buy another serving.

4 OUNCES CHOPPED CABBAGE

16 OUNCES RICE CAKE, CUT 2 INCHES LONG

2 OUNCES SCALLIONS, CHOPPED INTO 2-INCH STRIPS

2 OUNCES ONION, CUT INTO STRIPS

2 OUNCES CARROT, SHREDDED

¼ CUP WATER

sauce:

1 TABLESPOON SESAME OIL

2 TABLESPOONS SOY SAUCE

1 TEASPOON CRUSHED GARLIC

1 TEASPOON BROWN SUGAR

1 TEASPOON RED PEPPER FLAKES

1 TEASPOON RED PEPPER PASTE

In a cooking pot, mix together all the ingredients for the sauce. Add the cabbage, rice cakes, scallions, onion, carrot, and water and mix together. Cover and cook over a medium flame, stirring frequently. When the sauce thickens and the rice cakes feel soft, serve while hot.

SERVES 3 TO 4

떡
볶
이

Dumplings

Mandu

Dumplings are more complex to make than they seem. I remember watching my mother make them when I was young. She would mash the dough with her hands, slap some flour on it, then roll a bottle on it back and forth—it looked like fun.

I had made a few before she stopped me because I was overstuffing them. When she cooked the ones I made, they sprawled open in boiling water. She called me over to the pot to show me. "You see how it's not so easy to make them, but you could eat them up in a minute. Dumplings, like anything else, you become better at with practice."

To make them tasty, my mother's secret is to keep the filler a bit moist and the dough thin. (And, as I learned the hard way, don't overstuff!)

In some beef broth, dumplings also make a wonderful soup.

dough:

4 CUPS UNBLEACHED WHITE FLOUR
PINCH OF SALT
½ TEASPOON VEGETABLE OIL
1 EGG
¾ CUP WATER

stuffing:

1 POUND TOFU
10 OUNCES KIMCHI, MINCED
7 OUNCES SOYBEAN SPROUTS OR MUNG BEAN SPROUTS,
   BLANCHED AND MINCED
10 OUNCES GROUND BEEF
1 TABLESPOON MINCED SCALLION
1 TABLESPOON CRUSHED GARLIC
2 TABLESPOONS SESAME OIL
½ TEASPOON BLACK PEPPER
2 TABLESPOONS SESAME SALT
1 TEASPOON COARSE SALT
1 TEASPOON RED PEPPER

만
두

dipping sauce:

2 TABLESPOONS SOY SAUCE

1 TABLESPOON SESAME SEEDS

2 TEASPOONS RICE VINEGAR

1 TEASPOON RED PEPPER FLAKES

1. For the dough, combine flour, pinch of salt, oil, egg, and water in a large mixing bowl. Knead dough until smooth and free of lumps. Cover with a piece of damp cheesecloth and keep in a plastic bag. Let sit for 20 minutes. Meanwhile, prepare the stuffing.

2. Wrap the tofu in cheesecloth and squeeze out water. Do the same with the kimchi and bean sprouts. Combine all the stuffing ingredients in a mixing bowl and use your hands to blend thoroughly. Cover and keep aside.

3. Knead dough into a roll about 1½ inches in diameter. Cut the dough into ½-inch slices. With each slice, use a rolling pin, or a smooth glass bottle to roll out a thin skin. Rest the thinly rolled dough on your palm and delicately and neatly place a full teaspoon of stuffing in the center. Dabbing water on the perimeter of the skin, bring the skin over the stuffing. Seal by pinching the dough together and making sure that there are no air bubbles. Then take the two ends and make a curve, binding together with water. If you run out of dough, knead some more and keep the stuffing covered.

4. Cook the dumplings in boiling water. (They can also be fried or steamed, but I prefer my dumplings boiled.)

5. To make the dipping sauce, combine and stir the ingredients together. Serve the dumplings with the dipping sauce. Store any leftover dumplings in a freezer bag and keep them in the freezer for future servings.

SERVES 3 TO 4

Sautéed Korean Vermicelli with Vegetables

Japchae

In this dish, the vegetables are julienned to make them easier to pick up with chopsticks. Practical and easy to prepare, japchae is ideal for potluck parties and outings, or any kind of celebration, because it can easily be shared among a lot of people. It is tasty cold and does not need to be complemented with other side dishes. Furthermore, it's easy to transport because it is not soupy.

1 POUND GLASS NOODLES OR POTATO STARCH NOODLES
  (SEE PAGE 6)
3 OUNCES SCALLIONS, CUT INTO 1-INCH LENGTHS
3 OUNCES CARROT, JULIENNED
3 OUNCES ONION, JULIENNED
3 OUNCES MUSHROOMS, CUT INTO PIECES
7 OUNCES SPINACH, POACHED IN HOT WATER AND CUT INTO
  GENEROUS PIECES
1½ TABLESPOONS SOY SAUCE
1 TABLESPOON SESAME OIL
2 TEASPOONS CRUSHED GARLIC
3 TABLESPOONS BROWN SUGAR (OPTIONAL)
½ TEASPOON SESAME SEEDS

1. Soak the vermicelli in hot water for 15 minutes, then coarsely chop the vermicelli a few times for manageability.

2. Place vermicelli and all the vegetables, except the spinach, in a sauté pan. Add the soy sauce, sesame oil, garlic, and brown sugar and sauté over a medium flame for 4 or 5 minutes. Remove from flame and mix in the spinach while it is still hot. Sprinkle with sesame seeds.

SERVES 2 TO 3

A Spicy Summer Noodle Mix

Bibim gooksu

This noodle dish is very gratifying on hot summer days when you want to eat something light, healthy, and refreshingly cold. The crisp, clean texture of the cucumber combined with the spiciness from kimchi, the tang from the rice vinegar and a subtle sweetness from the sugar makes the dish so good. The noodles are served over a bed of ice, then topped with this spicy salad-like mixture.

2 FRESH CUCUMBERS, CUT INTO LONG, SKINNY SHREDS

10 OUNCES KIMCHI, CHOPPED COARSE WITH ITS JUICE

1 TABLESPOON SOY SAUCE

1 TABLESPOON SESAME OIL

1 TEASPOON CRUSHED GARLIC

1 TEASPOON SESAME SEEDS

1 TABLESPOON VINEGAR

1 TABLESPOON SUGAR

14 OUNCES KOREAN WHEAT-FLOUR NOODLES IN DRIED PASTA
    FORM

1. In a large mixing bowl, combine the cucumbers, kimchi, soy sauce, sesame oil, garlic, sesame seeds, vinegar, and sugar, using your hands to distribute the seasoning evenly. Keep aside.

2. Bring 10 cups of water to a boil, then add noodles. Cook for about 7 minutes, stirring to prevent clumping. Korean wheat-flour noodles are thin and cook fairly quick. Strain and run through cold water to chill.

3. Add the strained noodles to the salad mixture and mix roughly to dress the noodles. Put some ice in a shallow bowl, the noodles on top in a neat swirl, then use some of the salad mixture to spread over the top. Complement with Korean barley tea water to make the meal even more complete.

SERVES 3 TO 4

비

빔

국

수

Soups
(Gook)

子

Soups are my mom's comfort food, and her specialty in the kitchen. She has endless recipes and ingredients for soup all locked up in her mind. If soup is the main dish for dinner, she'll make something like yuke-jaong, which is a hearty and pungent shredded beef soup. And if it is a side dish, she'll prepare a broth-based refreshing light soup using bean sprouts, tofu, or sea kelp. Her soups never fail to hit the spot. Soup will always be my mom's favorite food. During the cold days of winter in Korea, she liked nothing more than a hot bowl of soup. For her, it is both nourishment and comfort.

My mother remembers very vividly the first dinner she ever cooked. She was around nine years old. Her mother was late coming home and it was getting dark outside. Soon it would be dinnertime and she did not know when her mother would return, so she took it upon herself to make dinner. She went outside to collect wood to start a fire and got water from the well. Mimicking what she had seen her mother do many times in the kitchen, she laid her palm on the bed of rice in water to measure how much water would be needed to cook the rice, up to the first knuckle. Then she started making the soup. Feeling like a very grown-up girl, she chopped the cabbage, as her mother would, distributing the soy bean paste through the boiling water and trying hard to remember what kind of seasoning her mother used. When my grandmother returned home, she was overwhelmed and delighted, and above all very proud. My grandfather was proud too when he was told who had made dinner. From then on, my grandmother started teaching my mother how to cook more and more each day.

Around the end of the Korean War, when my mother was six, her family fled south to seek a better life. With all the chaos, there was not enough food. Even if one had money to shop, the markets were always empty. There was no work yet because it was winter. The ground was frozen and there was no work in the fields either. The children could not go to school yet, but in the spring they could help with the planting in the fields. Those days in Nam-yang were simple: wake up, wash, eat breakfast, do the laundry, listen to the radio. In the afternoon the women would go out to the forest to collect plenty of wood to keep the fire burning. With fire, they kept warm and had hot water to cook and bathe.

That winter was the bleakest period of her family's life. For three cold months, they ate only twice a day. And my mother savored it. With the leafy parts of the cabbage that the neighbors gave my grandmother, she made a soup. To boiling broth of smooth soybean paste, my grandmother would add the bean sprouts and cabbage. With a tiny portion of rice, the family ate their meal. My mother remembers how good the soup tasted to her and how comforted it made her feel. The cabbage was so soft and the broth stimulated her appetite so that she had to eat slowly to make it last. My mother has never forgotten this soup. It was delicious—more memorable to her than anything else.

Soybean Sprout Soup

Chong-namul gook

This easy-to-make soup has medicinal qualities, ideal when you have a cold or a hangover. Along with some red pepper flakes, the spiciness will help you feel restored. And if you're experiencing a loss of appetite, this soup is light and quenching.

½ POUND SOYBEAN SPROUTS

3 CUPS WATER

1 TEASPOON CRUSHED GARLIC

½ TEASPOON COARSE SALT

1 TABLESPOON SOY SAUCE

¼ TEASPOON BEEF STOCK (OPTIONAL)*

2 OUNCES ONION, FINELY CHOPPED

5 OUNCES SCALLION, CUT INTO 1-INCH LENGTHS

Clean the soybean sprouts and strain. Place in a pot and add water, garlic, salt, soy sauce, dashida, and onion and cook for 7 to 10 minutes over a medium flame. Add scallions and bring to a boil. Serve hot.

SERVES 2 TO 3

*Beef stock can be substituted with 2 ounces of minced beef that can be added with the bean sprouts.

Napa Cabbage Soup

Baechu gook

12 OUNCES NAPA CABBAGE
4 OUNCES WHITE RADISH
4 OUNCES BEEF SHORT RIBS
4 OUNCES SCALLIONS
2 TABLESPOONS SOYBEAN PASTE (SEE PAGE 12)
6 CUPS WATER
1 TEASPOON RED PEPPER SAUCE (SEE PAGE 8)
2 TEASPOONS CRUSHED GARLIC

1. Clean the cabbage and shred with hands as desired, but in a wringing motion that will help soften the cabbage. Thinly slice the radish. Thinly slice the beef. Cut the scallions into 1-inch lengths.

2. In a pot, dissolve soybean paste in the water. For a smooth consistency, use a fine-mesh strainer with handle to remove the chunks of soybean paste floating in the soup and discard. Add the red pepper paste, cabbage, beef, radish, scallion, and garlic and cook for 7 minutes over a high flame, then for 3 more minutes over a medium flame. Serve hot with white rice, kimchi, and sautéed anchovy.

SERVES 3 TO 4

배
추
국

Alexandre Rockwell fell in love with the pork ribs just as my sister Jane did when she first sank her teeth into one. Ingredients (counterclockwise): sesame oil, brown sugar, ginger root slices, and minced garlic.

It was a treat when Mom brought home fresh crabs. Moon Sun and I loved to eat stewed crabs by mixing up little scoops of rice in the shells, smothered with the tasty sauce.

Snacks for drinking soju, Korean vodka, while playing Hatto, a Korean card game, are spicy sautéed squid with vegetables, panfried potatoes, and beefstuffed chili peppers served with a soy-and-vinegar dipping sauce.

Dad (second from right) and his friends liked to hang out by the shore with drinks and food. Among their favorites was the seafood pancake with Makalee, an unrefined version of rice wine that is milky in color.

Mom and Dad on their first hiking excursion together, around 1967. For outings like this, Mom made refreshing drinks like Shi'ke or Sujong gwa.

My mother, pictured here as a young woman (second from the right), loved to go out with her friends on the weekends. They'd stop to lunch on Nyeng-myun, a cold noodle soup in beef broth.

Hearty Kimchi Soup

Kimchi chi-gea

The spicy nature of this soup makes it especially good for congestion in the winter. If someone caught a bad cold, my mother prepared this soup for everyone to prevent others from catching the cold. Eating kimchi soup as fast as I did when I was a kid used to make me sweat furiously. But this was how I liked it. I always thought of it as a cleansing for my insides. After a hard day of work, my parents loved to eat it for dinner. Filling up on the rice steamed with beans that accompanies this soup to complete the meal, we felt very nourished.

Kimchi soup is very refreshing and intense in flavor if cooked properly. It is traditionally prepared with pork; however, it can also be made with beef or shrimp, or prepared with kimchi and tofu alone and it is just as good.

Prepare in bulk and keep refrigerated. Serve cold as well, over hot white rice.

1 POUND KIMCHI

2 TABLESPOONS SALAD OIL

1 TEASPOON CRUSHED GARLIC

7 OUNCES PORK, SLICED THIN (OPTIONAL)

1 CUP KIMCHI JUICE*

8 OUNCES TOFU, CUT INTO CUBES

4 OUNCES SCALLIONS, CUT INTO 1-INCH LENGTHS

1. Cut the kimchi into 1-inch squares. In a sauté pan, stir together the salad oil, garlic, pork, and kimchi for about 2 minutes. Then transfer the sauté to a pot.

2. Add the kimchi juice and 1 cup of water and bring to a boil. Finish off by adding tofu and scallions and bring to a boil once more. Serve hot.

SERVES 3 TO 4

김치
찌개

*Kimchi juice is the liquid in ripe kimchi. Juice from any of the kimchi described on pages 36–43 may be used.

Cold Cucumber Soup

Oye-neng gook

This cold cucumber soup is great to serve as a side dish for barbecued beef dishes, because it aids digestion. Clean, light, and refreshing, it is favored in the summer. It also activates your taste buds when you are feeling an appetite loss. Yet the best part about this soup is that it is delicious and so easy to prepare.

4 FRESH CUCUMBERS, SHREDDED LONG AND THIN
2 TABLESPOONS SOY SAUCE
2 TEASPOONS MINCED SCALLION
2 TEASPOONS RED PEPPER FLAKES
1 TABLESPOON VINEGAR
1 TEASPOON SESAME OIL
1 TEASPOON SESAME SEEDS
1 TEASPOON BROWN SUGAR
1 CUP OF ICE

In a big mixing bowl, mix together all the ingredients except the ice. Add the ice and mix again. Pour in 3 cups of water. Serve cold.

SERVES 3 TO 4

Fish and Tofu Soup

Mhe-un tang

1 TEASPOON BEEF STOCK

1 MEDIUM-SIZE TILEFISH, CUT INTO STEAKS, PLUS HEAD SPLIT
   OPEN

4 OUNCES TURNIP, OR RADISH, CUT UP INTO VERY THIN SLICES

4 OUNCES ONION, CHOPPED

2 TEASPOONS CRUSHED GARLIC

2 TEASPOONS SALT

1½ TABLESPOONS RED PEPPER FLAKES

1 BUNCH OF SCALLIONS, CUT INTO 1-INCH LENGTHS

1 TOFU CAKE, CUT INTO CUBES

8 OUNCES WATERCRESS

1. Bring 5 cups of water with the stock to a boil in a pot suitable to make soup.

2. Add the fish head, turnip, onion, garlic, salt, red pepper flakes, and bring to a boil again.

3. Add the fish steaks and bring to boil again until the fish is wholly cooked.

4. Finally, add in the scallions, tofu, and watercress. Without stirring, allow soup to simmer for 2 minutes. Serve hot.

SERVES 3 TO 4

매
운
탕

Noodles in Cold Beef Broth

Nyeng-myun

Nyeng-myun is a cold beef broth noodle soup that is eaten in the summertime. The occasion for us to have nyeng-myun was graduation. My mother always took us out to eat to celebrate. We always ordered nyeng-myun—it was too hot to eat anything else. Seasoning the soup to taste just right was the hard part—therefore, my mother had to season it for us. When I graduated from high school, I still couldn't season my soup right!

For a tasty broth, I like to add plenty of rice vinegar, hot mustard, and red pepper flakes. My mother's secret for making an even more flavorful soup broth is to combine the beef broth with some water kimchi juice. This is how nyeng-myun was originally made.

This cold noodle soup involves many steps, but the most essential part is a good broth. For the broth, it is important to know the parts. For every 3 cups of beef broth, use 3 cups of radish kimchi juice and combine it together with the seasonings. Prepare the broth first, and store it separate from the noodles until it is ready to go into a bowl. Add the hearty garnish last.

½ TO ¾ POUND SATAY BEEF (SEE PAGE 5)
3 CUPS RADISH KIMCHI JUICE (SEE PAGE 41)
1½ POUNDS BUCKWHEAT AND FLOUR NOODLES

seasonings:
4 TABLESPOONS RICE VINEGAR
2 TABLESPOONS HOT MUSTARD
2 TABLESPOONS BROWN SUGAR
1 TABLESPOON SALT
1 TEASPOON BEEF STOCK

garnish:
7 OUNCES RADISH KIMCHI
1 MEDIUM-SIZE KOREAN PEAR
2 FRESH KIRBY CUCUMBERS
4 HARD-BOILED EGGS

내
영
면

1. Prepare the broth. Halve the satay beef and boil with 5 cups of water for 20 minutes over a medium flame. Add 2 more cups of water and cook for 30 minutes over a low flame. Allow the broth to cool. As it cools, skim the fat from the surface. The beef broth is ready to be used. Reserve some of the beef used to make the broth for a garnish. Combine 3 cups of the beef broth with 3 cups of the kimchi juice. Mix in the seasonings. Chill the broth.

2. Prepare the noodles. In boiling water, cook the noodles for 2 to 3 minutes. The noodles will not clump if the water is hotter than 100 degrees. Strain and rinse through cold water. Put aside.

3. Prepare the garnish. It is faster and easier to use a shredder to cut the vegetables. Cut the kimchi and Korean pear into thin slices, almost transparent. Shred the cucumber, or chop fine. Slice the beef from the broth to use as garnish as well. Halve the eggs. Put aside.

4. Use a deep and wide bowl to serve this noodle soup. Make a swirl with the noodles and place in the bowl. Gently pour in the broth and, last, add the garnish.

5. At the table, have rice vinegar, hot mustard, and red pepper flakes ready for the guests to spice up their soup to taste.

SERVES 4

Seaweed Soup

Miyok gook

Just as American moms make chicken soup, Korean moms make seaweed soup. This soup, so simple and light with a very warm aroma, has healing power. The nutrients in this sea vegetable are known to help counteract the toxins in your blood. High in calcium and low in calories, this soup is good for hangovers and preventing blood clots.

Traditionally favored by mothers after giving birth, this soup is consumed ritually for a week to nurse back the robust spirit of the Korean mother. By my mother's side after giving birth, my grandmother would await with this soup. More generally, too, seaweed soup is frequently craved in the Korean household and eaten all the time.

Complement this soup with a bowl of white rice and some spicy side dishes, like kimchi. A Korean habit when eating this soup is drowning your rice in it, creating a heartier meal.

15 OUNCES DRIED SEAWEED (SEE PAGE 11)
7 OUNCES LEAN GROUND BEEF
1 TEASPOON CRUSHED GARLIC
PINCH OF BLACK PEPPER
1 TEASPOON SESAME OIL
2 TABLESPOONS SOY SAUCE
½ TEASPOON BEEF STOCK

1. Soak seaweed in water for about 10 minutes to rehydrate. Strain and cut the seaweed into 1½-inch-wide strips. Put aside.

2. In a mixing bowl, season the beef with garlic, black pepper, sesame oil, and 1 tablespoon of the soy sauce and mix together using your hands. Allow it to sit for 5 minutes.

3. In a pot suitable to cook soup, sauté the beef until it is partly cooked. Add the seaweed and sauté together for 2 minutes. Then add 7 cups of water and beef stock and cook for 10 minutes. Finish off by dashing in the remaining tablespoon of soy sauce.

SERVES 2 TO 3

미
역
국

Spinach and Clam Soup

Cho-gae tang

Complement this soup with white rice, kimchi, or other banchan to make a complete meal. It is also ideal to serve as a side soup with beef barbecues. Although it is good boiling hot, there is a cool sensation about the flavor of the broth from the clams.

1 DOZEN FRESH CHERRYSTONE CLAMS
1 POUND FRESH SPINACH
6 CUPS OF WATER
¼ TEASPOON BEEF STOCK
1½ TABLESPOONS SOYBEAN PASTE
4 OUNCES SCALLIONS, CUT INTO 1-INCH LENGTHS
1 TEASPOON CRUSHED GARLIC.

1. Soak the closed, fresh clams in salted water for about 20 minutes. Clams will naturally dispose of their residue in salty water, as if they were in the sea. It is important to do this because it is pretty unpleasant to bite into sand.

2. Clean spinach carefully, making sure to get all the dirt out. Blanch and run through cold water briskly. Coarsely chop. Put aside.

3. In a pot suitable to cook soup, combine the 6 cups of water and stock with the soybean paste to dissolve the paste. For an even soup, use a fine-mesh strainer with handle to remove the clumps. Add more soybean paste if you desire a darker broth.

4. Add the clams and bring to a boil. Then add the spinach, scallions, and garlic and bring to a boil again. Remove from heat right away and serve promptly.

SERVES 3 TO 4

Spicy Soft Tofu Soup

Suun-dubu

To make this soup, Koreans prefer to use a tukbae-gee, a traditional heatproof ceramic soup pot, because this pot will keep the soup hot even when it is removed from heat. If this pot is not available to you, any cooking pot will do and the soup will taste just as good.

5 TEASPOONS RED PEPPER FLAKES

2½ TEASPOONS SESAME OIL

2 TEASPOONS CRUSHED GARLIC

2 TEASPOONS SALT

9 OUNCES SOFT TOFU (SEE PAGE 13)

6 CHERRYSTONE CLAMS

½ TEASPOON BEEF OR CHICKEN STOCK

4 OUNCES CALAMARI OR SQUID, CUT INTO PIECES

4 OUNCES SHRIMP, CUT INTO PIECES

2 OUNCES SCALLIONS, CUT INTO 1-INCH LENGTHS

1. In a small skillet, combine 1 teaspoon red pepper flakes with ½ teaspoon of sesame oil and cook over a low flame. Keep aside and serve this sauce on the side when the soup is ready.

2. In a mixing bowl, combine 4 teaspoons red pepper flakes, the crushed garlic, salt, and 2 teaspoons sesame oil and mix together. Keep this mixture aside.

3. Using a heatproof ceramic soup pot, called tukbae-gee, or a cooking pot, combine 1 cup of water with the tofu, clams, and stock. Bring to a boil and when it boils add the calamari, shrimp, and scallions. Cook for 1 minute and remove from heat. Serve immediately with the sauce, even while the broth is still boiling in the tukbae-gee.

SERVES 2 TO 3

순
두
부

Beef Short Ribs in Broth

Kalbi tang

This soup can be eaten for a whole week and it will taste better each time. Just reheat the desired amount of broth and serve the sauce on the side for seasoning.

3 POUNDS BEEF SHORT RIBS (KALBI), CUT INTO 2 × 1-INCH
    PIECES
14 OUNCES WHITE RADISH, CUT INTO CUBES
1 TEASPOON SALT

sauce:
3 TABLESPOONS SOY SAUCE
1 TEASPOON RED PEPPER FLAKES
2 OUNCES SCALLIONS, MINCED
1 TEASPOON SESAME OIL
PINCH OF BLACK PEPPER
1 CHILI PEPPER OR JALAPEÑO PEPPER, MINCED

1. Soak the beef in water for 10 hours to take blood out. Change water after 5 hours and make sure to use an abundant amount of water. Remove the beef from water, place in a pot, and add enough water to cover the beef (the amounts of meat and water should be about equal). Bring to a boil. This helps to further remove the blood. After boiling, discard the water and rinse the beef in water.

2. Put the beef in a heavy pot and add 16 cups of water. Cook over medium heat for 20 minutes. Add cubed radish and 1 teaspoon salt. Cook for 10 more minutes.

3. Remove from heat and allow the broth to cool to room temperature, then refrigerate. Once the broth cools, skim the fat off the top with a spoon.

4. Mix all the ingredients together for the sauce and add to the soup when ready to be eaten. Complement with white rice and kimchi.

SERVES 4

갈비탕

Ginseng Chicken in Broth

Samgae-tang

The key to this chicken dish is the delicate method of preparation. I remember seeing my mother labor to get the soft meat to drip off the bones. To me, this was chicken soup, mild in seasoning but exuberant in flavor. My father and I considered it medicinal as we devoured this when I was kept home from school with the chicken pox. It turns out we were right, for the use of ginseng is the core of the recipe. The idiosyncrasy in this dish is that it is very popular during summertime. My mother's explanation is that during the summer it's hot, and we tend to sweat more, usually leaving us feeling dehydrated and fatigued. Therefore, in Korea, to help rejuvenate and nurture yourself back to shape, you eat this soup or take a steam bath, sweat out the toxins, cool down, and eventually feel stimulated and energized. Perhaps it is my mother's doing, but I find myself craving the stewed rice and chicken in broth with some cool kimchi on the hottest day of the summer.

2 CORNISH GAME HENS, OR ONE 2-POUND CHICKEN

½ CUP SWEET RICE

4 PIECES OF DRIED GINSENG ROOT

8 GARLIC CLOVES

10 RED DATES

9 CUPS WATER

1. Wash rice and put aside.

2. Clean out game hens or chicken thoroughly, discarding all guts; trim off the area around the cavity and discard the tail ends, which are the most odorous part. Scrub the insides clean while running through water. If using the two Cornish hens, divide the rice, ginseng, garlic, and dates to stuff the hens evenly. For a 2-pound chicken, combine all the ingredients for stuffing. Stuff loosely, keeping in mind that the rice will expand when it is cooked.

2. Use a heavy pot, good to make soup in, that will securely hold the two cornish hens. Place the stuffed Cornish hens into the pot, tucking in the flaps to prevent the stuffing from falling out. If you prefer to sew up the cavity, use a needle and thread or bind with a skewer stick. Usually tucking in the flap works only if the chicken fits securely in the pot. This chicken

dish is served in some broth and it gets messy trying to remove the thread when eating, so the other two methods are preferred.

3. Gently pour in 9 cups of water and cook for 30 minutes over a medium flame with a lid on. Skim the fat as the hens cook. After 30 minutes, the broth should have decreased by half, and the hens should be well cooked and tender. Poke to test with a fork. Cook for a few more minutes if necessary.

4. To serve, gently transfer the Cornish hens to a clay bowl to retain heat. It is optional to heat the clay bowl, if you are using a heatproof bowl. Add broth to cover about three quarters of the hens. Remember to inform your guests to discard the ginseng. Complement the soup with radish or cabbage kimchi.

SERVES 3 TO 4

Milky Bone Marrow Soup with Beef

Suhllun-tang

My mother had this soup ready for us to eat before we left for school. Having this hearty soup for breakfast during the cold winter months kept us energized as we stepped out into the cold and maneuvered our way through the snow. I think that feeding us this soup helped put my mother's mind at ease: as a working woman, she could go on her way, knowing that she had fed her children well.

Koreans love this soup's broth. The bone marrow is stewed for hours, forming a milky broth that is very rich and comforting. The beef and noodles are cooked separately, then combined and reheated before serving.

In Korea, suhllun-tang is traditionally stewed in enormous amounts that can last a whole family for a while. It is nourishing, plentiful in calcium and iron, and is loved by Korean elders and grown-ups alike. It is also good for growing children. Suhllun-tang is delicious served with rice and turnip kimchi. Koreans drown their rice in this soup to make it a heartier meal.

2½ POUNDS OF BONE MARROW CHUNKS

2 OUNCES SLICED GINGERROOT

18 OUNCES SATAY BEEF (SEE PAGE 5)

8 OUNCES KOREAN WHEAT-FLOUR NOODLES IN DRIED PASTA
    FORM

garnish:

¼ CUP MINCED SCALLION, ½ TEASPOON BLACK PEPPER, AND 1
    TEASPOON SESAME SALT, MIXED TOGETHER

seasoning:

SALT

RED PEPPER FLAKES

1. Make the broth:

First, soak overnight the bone marrow chunks in water to strain blood from them, while refrigerated. Then using an amount of water equivalent to the bone marrow, bring to a quick boil. This step will help get rid of odor in the bone marrow chunks. Then strain and wash bone marrow with water.

In a heavy pot, add 16 cups of water, the bone marrow, and ginger and cook over a high flame for 20 minutes. Then lower to medium flame and cook 10 minutes more. Then add 6 more cups of water and cook for 30 minutes over a medium flame. At this point the broth should be getting a cloudy consistency. Follow by adding 2 cups of water and cook over medium flame for another 30 minutes.

Allow the broth to cool in the pot. After it has cooled to room temperature, chill in the refrigerator. As the broth chills and condenses into a gelatinous form, the fat in the broth will rise to the surface. Skim with spoon. The broth is now ready for use. Prepare the beef and noodle separately, then later reheat in the broth before serving.

2. Cook the beef.

First, soak the beef in water for a couple hours to strain blood. In a pot, using an amount of water equivalent to the beef, cook for 40 minutes over medium flame. Check to see if the meat is done by poking into it with a fork. Discard the water. Allow the beef to cool down enough to make slicing it thin easy. Store on the side.

3. Prepare the noodle:

Bring 6 cups of water to a boil, add the noodles, and cook for about 7 minutes. Stir to avoid clumping. Do not over cook. Strain and store on the side.

4. To serve, use a separate pot and add the desired amount of broth, beef, and noodle. Use noodle in small amounts; suhllun-tang is not a noodle soup. Serve in deep clay bowls or a tukbae-ghee and add garnish. The salt and red pepper flakes should be served on the side, allowing the diner to add the seasoning according to taste.

SERVES 4

Fiery-Hot Beef Soup

Yuke-jaong

7 OUNCES GLASS NOODLES OR POTATO STARCH NOODLES (SEE
PAGE 6)

1½ POUNDS FLANK STEAK

8 CUPS BEEF BROTH, OR ½ TEASPOON DASHIDA DISSOLVED IN 8
CUPS WATER

2 TABLESPOONS SESAME OIL

1½ TABLESPOONS RED PEPPER FLAKES

1 TABLESPOON CRUSHED GARLIC

7 OUNCES SOYBEAN SPROUTS OR MUNG BEAN SPROUTS

2 TEASPOONS SALT

8 OUNCES SCALLIONS, CUT INTO 1-INCH LENGTHS

2 EGGS

1. Soak noodles in water and put aside.

2. Cook the flank steak in beef stock for 2 hours over a low flame. The broth should simmer until it is reduced to half. Skim fat as you go along. Remove beef from broth and put aside to cool, then shred with hands. Save the broth.

3. Make sauce to season the beef. In a small pan, combine sesame oil, red pepper flakes, and garlic and cook for 2 minutes over a low flame. Avoid burning the oil.

4. Mix the sauce with the beef and let it sit for 3 minutes.

5. Combine 4 cups of broth with the seasoned beef, sprouts, salt, scallions, and glass noodles and bring to a boil. When it boils, add eggs without stirring it too much. Serve hot.

6. Complement with water kimchi or pan-fried fish. This spicy soup is good for colds.

SERVES 3 TO 4

육개장

Rice Cake Soup

D'uk gook

7 OUNCES LEAN BEEF
4 CUPS BEEF BROTH, OR ¼ TEASPOON DASHIDA DISSOLVED IN 4
    CUPS WATER (SEE PAGE 1)
1½ POUNDS RICE CAKES
10 DUMPLINGS (OPTIONAL)
1 TEASPOON SALT
2 EGGS
2 TABLESPOONS MINCED SCALLIONS
PINCH OF BLACK PEPPER
2 TABLESPOONS SESAME SEEDS
TOASTED SEAWEED, CRUMBLED (OPTIONAL)

1. Chop the beef into pieces and soften by beating it with the blunt side of a knife. In a pot, bring the 4 four cups of beef broth to a boil with the beef.

2. Add the rice cakes and dumplings with 1 teaspoon of salt. When the soup begins to boil again, break in the eggs and simmer until the egg is done.

3. Season with the minced scallions, black pepper, sesame seeds, and toasted seaweed, if available. Serve immediately, and complement with radish kimchi.

SERVES 2 TO 3

떡
국

Meat, Chicken, and Fish
(Gogi)

고기 닭 생선

My earliest memories of growing up in Queens are Sunday barbecues with my family, and especially that unforgettable smell of Korean beef marinade grilling in open air. My mother had the important task of preparing the beef—the main course. Her beef marinade was the best; my aunts didn't even prepare theirs, because everyone would only eat Mom's.

With our cooler filled with soda, a bamboo mat, a portable grill, and lots of food my mother had prepared and stored in plastic containers, as well as a whiffle bat and ball, we were ready to go. We would load everything into the van and drive over to Kissena Park to meet our relatives for an afternoon barbecue.

BULGOGI AND KALBI

Bulgogi is translated as "fire meat." This refers to the way the meat is cooked, first marinated, then grilled over hot coals or an open fire. At home, we often used a portable gas grill as opposed to the frying pan to cook the bulgogi. The grill was set in the middle of our dining table and everyone at the table reached over and ate the beef right off the grill. The table was filled with bowls of banchan, rice, and fresh greens like red leaf lettuce, perilla leaves, and chrysanthemum leaves.

Kalbi preparation is similar to bulgogi preparation, except the beef tends to be more tender and fattier around the bone. Kalbi is made with beef short ribs. It is cut thicker than bulgogi, therefore the marinating takes longer, and as a result, the flavor is more potent and sweeter. Kalbi need not be served with fresh greens or the soybean paste dip sauce, although many prefer it that way. I like eating kalbi with some crisp and cool "bachelor kimchi" for a maximum contrast in flavor.

You can prepare bulgogi or kalbi in large quantities, marinate it, and cook the amount you desire to serve for dinner. My mother used to marinate 6 to 7 pounds of beef to last a whole week. In any household, bulgogi is a convenient and quick beef dish to prepare and is ideal to whip up for dinner.

My mother often used her hand to blend in the sauce when she prepared kalbi. Once I hovered over her mixing bowl and asked, "Why do you use your hands?" She replied, "Because that way, I can season everything evenly and I can't miss the spots that I'd miss if I used a fork.

Korean Barbecue Beef, MARINADE 1

Bulgogi

As you will see when you are barbecuing this marinated beef, its smell will make your mouth water. Once you try Korean barbecue, it will become something you crave—even if you're not usually a beef eater.

Bulgogi is traditionally eaten with white rice and a variety of sides, usually spicy ones. Most important, serve it with fresh red leaf lettuce, thinly sliced raw garlic, and some spicy fresh peppers to make a ssam: *holding the lettuce in your palm, make a wrap that envelops the barbecued beef, some rice, the dipping sauce, and, if desired, the vegetables. Feel free to experiment!*

2½ POUNDS RIB EYE BEEF, THINLY SLICED
2 TABLESPOONS SOY SAUCE
2 TEASPOONS SESAME OIL
2 TEASPOONS CRUSHED GARLIC
2 TABLESPOONS BROWN SUGAR
1 TABLESPOON RICE WINE (SAKE)
PINCH OF BLACK PEPPER
½ PIECE OF FRESH KIWI, JUICED IN A BLENDER

dipping sauce:
1 TABLESPOON SOYBEAN PASTE
1 TEASPOON CRUSHED GARLIC
2 TEASPOONS RED PEPPER SAUCE (SEE PAGE 8)
1 TEASPOON SALAD OIL
2 TABLESPOONS WATER

1. Trim the fat off the beef with a knife. Distribute the sugar evenly on the beef by sprinkling it on each piece. Allow beef to sit for 10 minutes.

2. In a separate bowl, mix together the soy sauce, sesame oil, garlic, sugar, sake, and black pepper. Put aside.

3. Massage the beef with the kiwi juice using your hands. The kiwi works as a tenderizer. Add the soy sauce mixture and mix. Allow the beef to marinate for 10 minutes. Because the beef is thin, it doesn't require a long marinating time. Now it is ready to be barbecued. Ideal if grilled over

불고기

smoked wood but just as good in a frying pan or skillet. Cook until browned, being careful not to overcook.

4. Last, to prepare dipping sauce, combine all sauce ingredients and cook over low heat for 15 to 20 minutes. Serve on the side.

SERVES 3 TO 4

AWAY FROM HOME

It's always when we love something we realize how much we've taken it for granted. I never really considered family time to be important until I left for college. Time spent together in our family was always dinner. It was the one time during the day that we would actually sit down to be together. Everyone was so busy. Dinner was a feast with plenty of food to enjoy. Mom would cook so much of her delicious dishes that none of us stopped after just one bowl of rice. Even if I was stuffed, I'd help myself to another serving. My favorite was always the kalbi, which she cooked almost four times a week. But I would eat anything Mom cooked. It's her selection of the finest, freshest ingredients and perfect balance of flavor that makes all the difference.
—Moon Sun Kwak

Korean Barbecue Beef, MARINADE 2

Kalbi

1 POUND BEEF SHORT RIBS, CUT FOR KALBI (SEE PAGE 5)
2 TABLESPOONS BROWN SUGAR
2 TABLESPOONS SOY SAUCE
2 TEASPOONS SESAME OIL
2 TEASPOONS CRUSHED GARLIC
1 TABLESPOON RICE WINE (SAKE)
PINCH OF BLACK PEPPER
½ PIECE OF FRESH KIWI, JUICED IN A BLENDER

1. Distribute the sugar evenly on the beef short ribs by sprinkling it on each piece. Allow beef to sit for 10 minutes.

2. In a bowl, mix together soy sauce, sesame oil, garlic, sake, and black pepper. Put aside.

3. Massage the beef with the kiwi juice using your hands. The kiwi works as a tenderizer. Add the sauce and mix. Allow the beef to marinate for 2 hours before barbecuing.

SERVES 2

Pork Marinade for Barbecue

Daeji-bulgogi

1 POUND LEAN AND BONELESS PORK, CUT INTO THIN SLICES

marinade:
3 TABLESPOONS SOY SAUCE
2 TABLESPOONS CRUSHED GARLIC
½ TEASPOON CRUSHED GINGERROOT
2 TABLESPOONS BROWN SUGAR
2 TABLESPOONS RED PEPPER SAUCE
1 TEASPOON RED PEPPER FLAKES
2 TABLESPOONS RICE WINE (SAKE)
2 TABLESPOONS SESAME OIL

Combine all the ingredients for the marinade and stir in a large mixing bowl. Add the pork and marinate for 10 minutes. Ready to grill.

SERVES 2 TO 3

돼지불고기

Beef Barbecue with Sesame-Salt Dipping Sauce

Loosugui

Among the various types of Korean barbecue, loosugui is best known as the non-marinade beef barbecue. Using the same prime beef used for bulgogi, the thin slices of beef are cooked unseasoned and eaten dipped into an aromatic sauce made with sesame oil, salt, and black pepper. Take a piece of the beef hot off the grill or skillet and dip. The beef is also traditionally complemented with a crisp, sharp scallion salad.

With the accompaniment of rice wines—jong-jan, *a refined rice wine, or* makalee, *a milky rice wine—this is a popular dish to share with friends.*

Loosugui is popular all year round, cooked on a portable burner at the center of the table. We ate loosugui with side dishes like sweet-vinegar turnip salad, cucumber salad, and marinated soybeans. It was also even more delicious to eat the beef and scallion salad using leafy greens like red leaf lettuce, minty perilla leaves, and bitter chrysanthemum leaves to make a wrap, or ssam.

1 POUND BEEF RIB EYE, THINLY SLICED

1. Present the raw beef on a platter if grilling at the table. Garnish with fresh mushrooms and sliced garlic cloves.

2. If grilling in a skillet, cook the beef in an ungreased pan over a medium flame. Lay the slices of beef flat in the pan and do not overlap. You may need to do more than one batch, depending on the size of your skillet. The thin slices of beef cook fairly quickly, so be careful not to overcook. Garnish is optional if cooking in a skillet.

3. Have the dipping sauce and scallion salad already prepared at the table so you can enjoy the beef while it is still hot.

dipping sauce:
FOR 1 TABLESPOON OF SESAME OIL, USE 2 TABLESPOONS OF SALT AND A PINCH OF BLACK PEPPER AND MIX. MAKE AS MUCH OF THE SAUCE AS YOU LIKE USING THESE PROPORTIONS.

로스구이

scallion salad:

2 TEASPOONS SOY SAUCE

1 TEASPOON SUGAR

1 TEASPOON SESAME SALT

½ TEASPOON CRUSHED GARLIC

1 TEASPOON RICE VINEGAR

½ TEASPOON RED PEPPER FLAKES

1 BUNCH OF SCALLIONS, SHREDDED

Soak the shredded scallions in water for 15 minutes to help decrease the oniony pungency. Strain. In a mixing bowl, add all the seasonings and mix together gently, using your hands to distribute the seasonings evenly. Serve right away; the scallion tends to wilt quickly.

SERVES 2 TO 3

Stewed Beef Ribs

Kalbi jjim

4 POUNDS BEEF SHORT RIBS
3 TABLESPOONS MINCED GARLIC
1½ CUPS SOY SAUCE
3 TABLESPOONS SESAME OIL
4 TABLESPOONS BROWN SUGAR
3 TABLESPOONS RED PEPPER FLAKES
4 OUNCES GINGERROOT, SLICED INTO LENGTHWISE PIECES
3 CUPS WATER
PINE NUTS FOR GARNISH
THREADED RED PEPPER FOR GARNISH (OPTIONAL)

1. Cut grooves into the kalbi meat and cut off excess fat. Boil the meat in water to help get rid of the beef odor before stewing. Discard the water and wash the beef with warm water.

2. In a heavy pot, combine the kalbi with garlic, soy sauce, sesame oil, sugar, red pepper flakes, and ginger and mix together using a spoon. Add the water and mix once more.

3. Cook over a high flame for 7 minutes, covered. Continue to cook for 30 minutes over a medium flame. Because kalbi tends to be fatty, it is good to skim the surface of fat as it cooks. By now the beef should be well cooked and tender. If not, allow it to cook for a few minutes. Discard the ginger and garnish with pine nuts and threaded red pepper. Serve hot.

4. Store the leftovers in the refrigerator for future servings. Stewed beef ribs will keep for a week.

SERVES 3 TO 4

갈비찜

Spicy Pork Ribs

Daeji-kalbi

5 POUNDS PORK RIBS

4 OUNCES GINGERROOT, SLICED INTO LENGTHWISE PIECES

3 CUPS WATER

3 TABLESPOONS MINCED GARLIC

1½ CUP SOY SAUCE

3 TABLESPOONS SESAME OIL

4 TABLESPOONS BROWN SUGAR

3 TABLESPOONS RED PEPPER FLAKES

1. Cut grooves in the pork meat and cut off excess fat. Boil the pork ribs in water to get rid of the pork odor before stewing. Discard the water and wash the ribs through warm water.

2. In a heavy pot, bring the pork ribs to a boil with the ginger and water. When it boils, add the garlic, soy sauce, sesame oil, sugar, and red pepper flakes. Stir together using a spoon. Cook over a high flame for 7 minutes, covered. Continue to cook for 20 minutes over a medium flame. Because pork ribs tends to be fatty, it is good to skim the surface of fat as it cooks. By now the ribs should be well cooked and tender. If not, allow it to cook for a few minutes, covered.

3. Discard the ginger before serving.

SERVES 3 TO 4

돼지갈비

One Hundred Eighty Degrees
Jane Kwak

Above her chafed arms, her forearms are as alabaster, smooth and very pale. She has that Asian gift of fair skin with pores so tight that water dances off her wet arms. Her small hands exude warmth.

Her eyes are doe-like, not the narrow almond type. There's a shininess in her eyes even if she has been standing all day. Although she spends most of her day in the kitchen, although she is hidden from customers, and although it is the florid young waitresses whom the people see, it is the short and weary woman who opened and owns the restaurant.

Most of her customers who have a fancy for her cooking are young city inhabitants. Their favorite, they tell me, is the broiled pot chicken. Even if their unaccustomed tongues cannot tolerate the generous helping of red pepper, their grimace is interpreted as delight. It is amusing that many people take such an interest in what is to us Korean house cooking.

When she opened the restaurant she took a chance. That was nearly three years ago. It has been three years of hugging her as I detect traces of food absorbed by her hair; it has also been three years of not seeing her for several days at a time; and it has been three years of eating out or alone. It is hard because she is the main chef and the owner, so I see her less often as the restaurant gets busier. There are three others who can help her with the increased work, but she insists on handling the matters personally. "How could they manage?" she questions. Although they have worked together for three years, they do still need her. As I see the restaurant growing, I realize the wisdom of her decisions.

I don't know where we would be had she not opened the restaurant. We had experienced drought not only of money but of hope. I know it hurt her and scared her the most - but she didn't show it. In Korea, she had married well; she didn't expect to come to America to be a working Korean lady. All her assets resided in being a mother, preparing mounds of dumplings for her querulous children. She came to America knowing nothing other than her name in English. She acquired various jobs to support us as children. She began by studying styles of cooking and improving her own. Then she made the premeditated decision to open her own restaurant. She overcame her fears and gambled with the little security she had to fulfill her decision. She rejected the role of woman that had been taught to her. She was able to change, and she achieved success through hard work. She taught this to me, her daughter.

And down in the Lower East Side, as the sreetlights flick on, and the restaurant opens, people crowd into the restaurant. I too join them with the comforting thought of my mother, the source of all that I am and hope to become, working diligently in the kitchen.

Stewed Chicken with Potatoes

D'ak-dori-tang

I bungled the recipe when I first attempted to make this dish. I read "tablespoon" for teaspoon and put in two heaping tablespoons of sugar. It was tasty, but strangely sweet. I suppose all great chefs have to begin somewhere . . .

Sweet or not, remember to cut the potatoes a bit smaller than the chicken, so they will be tender when the chicken is done.

1 POUND BONELESS CHICKEN THIGH MEAT, CUT INTO 1-INCH CHUNKS

2 MEDIUM POTATOES, CUT INTO 1-INCH CUBES

1 ONION, CHOPPED

2 TABLESPOONS RED PEPPER FLAKES

2 TEASPOONS CRUSHED GARLIC

2 TEASPOONS SUGAR

3 TABLESPOONS SOY SAUCE

1 TABLESPOON RICE WINE (SAKE)

2 TEASPOONS SESAME OIL

½ CUP WATER

4 OUNCES SCALLIONS, CUT INTO 1-INCH LENGTHS

1. In a heavy pot, combine the chicken with the potatoes, onion, red pepper flakes, garlic, sugar, soy sauce, rice wine, and sesame oil. Mix together, then add ½ cup of water and mix again. Cover and cook for 20 minutes over a medium flame.

2. Add the scallions and cook for 3 more minutes. Serve hot.

SERVES 2 TO 3

닭
도
리
탕

Spicy Stewed Crab

Gea-jorim

4 FRESH CRABS, LIVE AND HEAVY IN WEIGHT
1 TEASPOON GINGER JUICE
4 GREEN KOREAN CHILI PEPPERS, HALVED AND CUT INTO 1-INCH
    LENGTHS
4 OUNCES SCALLIONS, CUT INTO 1-INCH LENGTHS
2 TEASPOONS CRUSHED GARLIC
2 TABLESPOONS RED PEPPER SAUCE (SEE PAGE 8)
2 TEASPOONS SOYBEAN PASTE
2 TABLESPOONS SOY SAUCE
1 TABLESPOONS SALAD OIL
1 CUP WATER
½ BUNCH WATERCRESS

1. Clean the crabs. Remove the shells but save to use in stew. Discard the guts and rinse with water. Cut off the pointy ends of the claws. Crack the legs once using a blunt object. Then cut up the crab into 4 parts (6 parts if the crab is big). Keep aside.

2. Mix together the ginger juice, peppers, scallions, garlic, red pepper paste, soybean paste, soy sauce, and salad oil. Add the water and stir until the sauce appears to be even.

3. In a heavy pot, put in the crabs and the reserved shells. Pour the sauce over them, then cover and cook over a medium flame until the crab is well cooked. The inside of the crab will appear white and the crab should feel softer when you poke with a fork. Lastly, add the watercress and simmer for 1 minute. Serve immediately.

4. Complement the dish with white rice, a mildly seasoned selection of side dishes or a fresh salad, and, of course, some kimchi.

SERVES 2 TO 3

계
조
림

Spicy Stewed Fish and Radish

Seng-sun jorim

½ POUND RADISH, CHOPPED INTO ¼-INCH CUBES

2 POUNDS FRESH KINGFISH STEAKS OR SPANISH MACKEREL
   STEAKS

3 KOREAN CHILI PEPPERS, CUT COARSELY

½ CUP SOY SAUCE

2 TABLESPOONS BROWN SUGAR

2 TABLESPOONS CRUSHED GARLIC

2 TABLESPOONS RED PEPPER SAUCE (SEE PAGE 8)

2 TABLESPOONS RED PEPPER FLAKES

3 TABLESPOONS SALAD OIL

½ TEASPOON BEEF STOCK

4 OUNCES SCALLIONS, CUT INTO 1-INCH LENGTHS

1 MEDIUM ONION, CUT INTO STRIPS

¾ CUP WATER

1. In a heavy pot suitable to stew, arrange the chopped radish on the bottom, then lay the fish on top. Keep aside.

2. In a bowl, stir together the chili peppers, soy sauce, brown sugar, garlic, red pepper flakes, red pepper paste, salad oil, dashida, chopped scallions, and the onion. Mix in the water.

3. Spread the sauce mixture over the fish but do not stir in. Reserve some of the sauce. Cover and cook the fish over a medium-high flame for 7 minutes. Then over a low flame, continue to cook for 10 more minutes.

4. Gently place the fish and radish on a plate and spread extra sauce over the fish. Serve with hot rice and some side dishes like marinated soybeans, seasoned soybean sprouts, and kimchi.

SERVES 4

생선 조림

Stuffed Zucchini (with Beef)

Hobak jjim

One of the simpler stewed beef and vegetable recipes, stuffed zucchini is a hearty, satisfying dish. Passed on to my mother by her mother from her grandmother, it has long been a favorite among the women of our family.

When my mother was a girl, Kaesong, a region in central-west Korea (now part of North Korea), swarmed with merchants and their wives and children. The region produced celebrated cooks—among them, my mother informs me, my great-grandmother. She was sought after to cater this particular dish for weddings and birthday ceremonies. Recipes were not recorded back then; to be a great cook was considered a gift. Luckily, the recipe survived.

4 ZUCCHINI

14 OUNCES GROUND BEEF

3 TABLESPOONS SOY SAUCE

1 TEASPOON SESAME OIL

⅓ TEASPOON BLACK PEPPER

2 TEASPOONS CRUSHED GARLIC

2 TEASPOONS OF SUGAR

2 TABLESPOONS RICE WINE (SAKE)

½ CUP WATER

sauce:

2 TABLESPOONS SOY SAUCE

2 TEASPOONS RICE VINEGAR

½ TEASPOON RED PEPPER FLAKES

1 TEASPOON SESAME SEEDS

1. Wash zucchini, lightly scrubbing off all dirt. Then cut the zucchini into thirds. At the end of each piece make two grooves with a knife, forming a criss-cross.

2. Tenderize the beef by pounding on it with the dull side of your knife. Combine the beef, soy sauce, sesame oil, black pepper, garlic, sugar, and sake. Using your hands, mix in a massaging motion to distribute the seasoning evenly.

호
박
찜

3. Stuff the beef into the zucchini generously without breaking the zucchini. Then place it in a cooking pot neatly as you go along. Spread the leftover beef over the zucchini.

4. Gently pour the water into the pot. Cover the pot and cook over a medium flame for 15 minutes. Turn over zucchini and let them cook for 10 more minutes.

5. While the beef cooks, mix all the ingredients for the sauce together and stir. Place zucchini on a plate and evenly distribute the sauce on the stuffed zucchini with a teaspoon just before serving.

Serves 3 to 4

Beef Stewed in Soy Sauce

Jang-jorim

This is sometimes served as a side dish.

1 POUND FLANK STEAK
3 PIECES OF GINGER
5 CUPS WATER
1 CUP SOY SAUCE
½ CUP BROWN SUGAR
12 GARLIC CLOVES (PEEL AND USE WHOLE)
6 KOREAN TWIST PEPPERS, WHOLE (SEE PAGE 7)

1. Boil beef in water, strain, and wash with warm water. Cool and cut into chunks about 1½ inches square.

2. Combine beef and ginger with 5 cups of water, cover, and cook for 30 minutes over a medium flame. Skim the fat from the surface as it cooks. After 30 minutes, the water should be reduced to half the amount you started with. Add soy sauce, sugar, and garlic and cook for 20 minutes over a low-medium flame. Add peppers and cook for 5 minutes, covered. Discard the ginger but serve the garlic and peppers with the soy sauce beef. Keep refrigerated for up to a week.

SERVES 3 TO 4

Spicy Squid Sautéed with Vegetables

Ojinx-o bokum

There is a Korean saying that spicy food relieves stress. The spicier the dish the better, and this one is definitely spicy. It makes a good party dish, popular among men, who complement it with a cold bottle of soju, Korean vodka. My mother would prepare this dish for my father when he had company, and the men would socialize, drinking the vodka, laughing and talking. No one seemed too stressed!

1 POUND MEDIUM-SIZE FRESH SQUID

4 OUNCES SCALLIONS, CUT INTO 1-INCH LENGTHS

4 OUNCES CARROTS, CUT INTO JULIENNE

5 OUNCES ONIONS, CUT INTO JULIENNE

4 OUNCES MUSHROOMS, CHOPPED

4 OUNCES SPICY KOREAN PEPPERS, CHOPPED

2 TABLESPOONS VEGETABLE OIL

2 TEASPOONS CRUSHED GARLIC

1 TEASPOON SALT

2 TABLESPOONS RED PEPPER FLAKES

2 TEASPOONS BROWN SUGAR (OPTIONAL)

1. Clean and cut squid into flat 1 x 2-inch pieces.
2. In a pot suitable to sauté, place squid and all the vegetables on top. Add the oil, garlic, salt, red pepper flakes, and sugar and sauté over a high flame for 4 minutes, or until squid is tender (do not overcook). Remove from heat right away. Serve hot.

SERVES 2

오징어 볶음

Mom's Spicy Drumsticks

Dak-jorim

On weekends when my mother stayed home from work, she spent her time cooking, and sometimes inventing new dishes. One of her successful recipes is this version of fried chicken, whisked with a spicy and sweet jalapeño sauce. Four small quarters of jalapeño peppers make all the difference in this dish. The slivers of pepper are simmered to make the sauce, and carefully basted on the fried chicken right before serving. The chicken stayed crispy and the sauce was so appetizing that we became addicted, and the dish became part of my mom's repertoire. Try this recipe using breast meat as well.

A deep fryer is ideal for this recipe (a portable one is fine).

1½ POUNDS CHICKEN DRUMSTICKS
PINCH OF SALT
½ TEASPOON BLACK PEPPER
½ MEDIUM ONION, JUICED IN A BLENDER
VEGETABLE OIL FOR FRYER

batter:
½ CUP WATER
2 CUPS FLOUR, PLUS EXTRA TO COAT CHICKEN
2 EGGS

sauce:
½ CUP SOY SAUCE
6 PIECES OF JALAPEÑO PEPPERS, HALVED
3 TABLESPOONS BROWN SUGAR
2 TABLESPOONS WATER

1. Prepare chicken by discarding the skin and cutting grooves in the chicken. Sprinkle the salt and pepper evenly on chicken. Use half the onion juice to marinate the chicken for 10 minutes.

2. Meanwhile, combine all the ingredients for the sauce and mix using a spoon. In any small pot, bring it to a quick boil and keep aside.

3. Mix the batter using ½ cup water, the flour, eggs, and remaining onion juice.

4. Fill half the fryer with vegetable oil and heat until the oil gets very hot. When ready to fry the chicken, sprinkle a thin layer of flour on chicken. Dip the drumsticks into the batter and gently shake off the excess. Cook the chicken at 350 degrees for 5 to 10 minutes.

4. Brush sauce on fried chicken, or gently pour the sauce over the chicken. Serve immediately.

SERVES 3 TO 4

Salted Fish Bake

Seng-sun gui

Arriving home, I knew what we were having for dinner some nights from the aroma lingering around the building. Especially when my mother baked or fried fish. The smell was quite pervasive—and delicious.

Our family ate the fish to the bone—that's how much we savored it. It was almost disreputable for a Korean not to know how to eat a fish properly; the only thing left should be the bone. My mother always had the honor of paring off the main bone, the tastiest part of the fish. My father dug in to pick up chunks of meat once the bone was gone, and my sisters and I did the same. We placed the fish in our bowls of rice. If we picked up parts with ka-shi (bone) in it, we had to remove it before we could eat it. Holding the chopsticks as steady as possible so that we didn't drop the goods, we picked the ka-shi out with our free hand. Eating fish was quite a task, but delicious. It's definitely easier for adults!

4 MACKEREL, CLEANED AND SPLIT
1 TABLESPOON COARSE SALT

dipping sauce:
4 TABLESPOONS SOY SAUCE
1 TEASPOON SESAME SEEDS
1 TEASPOON RED PEPPER FLAKES
1 TEASPOON CRUSHED GARLIC
1 TEASPOON MINCED SCALLION
1 TEASPOON BROWN SUGAR
1 TABLESPOON RICE VINEGAR

1. Distribute the sea salt generously over the fish and leave uncovered in refrigerator overnight or for a day.

2. Bake the fish in a 300-degree oven until it is fully cooked.

3. Mix all the ingredients for dipping sauce. Serve the sauce on the side. Serve with white rice and roasted seaweed laver.

SERVES 4

생
선
구
이

Party Snacks and Little Dishes

(Ganshik and Anjou)

간식 과 안주

Ganshik are best described as snacks or little dishes. Anjou are party snacks, foods that accompany alcoholic beverages.

Fueled by bottles of Korean vodka called *soju* (made from sweet potatoes), beer, and scotch, after-dinner Korean poker games in our house could last for hours. It was a matter of time until my mom started making scallion pancakes, or cooking sun-dried cuttlefish over open flames, to accompany drinks during the game. As boisterous or solemn the players may have seemed in contemplating their next moves, they were chewing on tasty bite-size zucchini fillets or squid seasoned in chili sauce. Spicy anjou were favored because they activated the taste buds, and mild anjou were served to help the players fill up while drinking.

With or without the poker game, these anjou are a delicious addition to any gathering.

ROLLING KIMBOP

Kimbop, a seaweed roll of rice, beef, and seasoned vegetables, was one of my favorite snacks as a little girl. Koreans love kimbop, and my mother made it for me often. She never made just a couple—it was always a pile of kimbop. It all happened on our dining room table. She'd set up all the ingredients she needed to roll an army-batch. With hot rice still steaming in the rice cooker, a bowl of seasoned spinach and shredded carrots, a plate of duakuan strips, a pan of ground bulgogi beef, and oodles of egg strips, she was almost ready to start rolling. On a cutting board, she would spread out layers of kim—*seaweed sheets—to soften the surface on which she would roll the kimbop. Back then she did not have the aid of a bamboo roller; she used her palm and fingers to gently guide and tightly make a roll. My mother was very skilled at this. She worked at a quick pace and all the rolls turned out perfectly. With just the right proportion of ingredients, her rolls had a consistent thickness and were the most appetizing. It is important to remember that spreading too much rice, or having an uneven amount of vegetables, could ruin the kimbop. I learned this by trial and error.*

After having watched her make a few rolls, I sat at the table wondering if I could master it too. It seemed simple enough. Gulping down a piece of kimbop, I set up a little station like hers. On my seaweed sheet, I dropped a scoop of rice and started spreading it out with my fingers as she did, occasionally dipping my fingers into some water to help separate the rice.

"That's too much rice," she said.

"No, it's not. It'll be fine, I know what to do," I barked.

She let me continue and I tried to follow her arrangement with the vegetables, except my fingers were stuck with rice and I couldn't get it to stay on the sheet of seaweed. I started flicking my fingers around trying to shake off the rice. Then I started lining up the vegetables on my bed of rice. A row of beef, spinach, carrot, egg, duakuan. I lined up some extra spinach and egg strips in the roll—customizing my kimbop since I liked these ingredients the best.

"You're going to have a hard time rolling that," she warned.

I started rolling it up, lifting the end carefully and folding it over. I was doing fine. I could already tell that my roll would be a bit thicker, so I started pressing it in a little harder while making a complete rotation. I saw the seaweed sheet tear in some areas. But it couldn't tear too much, I thought, so I kept working.

A dab of water is used to bind the loose end of the seaweed. But even a small drop of water can be too much sometimes. To avoid over-wetting the seaweed, it is safer to use a hint of moisture. A tiny dab on the fingertips is enough.

Carefully I managed to wet the seaweed enough to stick, but a second later, it separated. I heard my mother giggle so I dampened it more. When that didn't really work I covered it up by putting the seam face down on the cutting board. My mother, ready to slice my rice roll, slowly wiped her knife with a wet cloth for a really clean cut. She delicately slid her knife through and by the time she started cutting the rice roll for the second piece, the kimbop unraveled before our eyes.

"You didn't listen to me," my mother teased. She tried to fix the roll enough to cut into pieces. Handing me my plate of unrolled kimbop, my mother said I had to eat it. That day I realized I should spend more time listening to the advice of an experienced mom before I give myself credit for knowing more than I actually do.

Seaweed Roll of Rice and Vegetables

Kimbop

You will need a bamboo roller to make these seaweed rolls.

8 SHEETS OF SEAWEED, EACH 8 INCHES SQUARE

1½ CUPS RICE, COOKED AND READY TO USE

8 OUNCES OF VINEGAR-PICKLED DUAKUAN (SEE PAGE 2 FOR
    DESCRIPTION)

2 OUNCES SEASONED SPINACH (SEE PAGE 17)

4 OUNCES BULGOGI BEEF (SEE PAGE 5)

2 EGGS, MIXED AND COOKED INTO A THIN SHEET, THEN CUT INTO
    SHREDS

2 OUNCES OF CARROT, SHREDDED AND BLANCHED

1. Have all the ingredients to make kimbop ready before rolling. Have everything in separate bowls to make your work convenient, and work on a spacious table. Also have a little saucer of water available to wet your fingers. Halve the duakuan lengthwise. Using half of it, slice into 8 thin strips; keep the other half refrigerated. Serve the leftover duakuan cut into thin slices on the side with the kimbop rolls.

2. On a cutting board, lay down a sheet of seaweed. Using a rice ladle, place one scoop of rice on the seaweed and evenly spread it out using your fingers. Wet your fingers to help you spread out the rice. Covering about half the seaweed sheet with rice, make sure the layer of rice is even, and skimpy rather then heavy. If you have too much rice on the seaweed, take some out.

3. Place a strip of the duakuan in the center of the rice, then line up a thin row of egg, beef, spinach, carrot as well in any order. Just remember to keep the rows thin. Taking the end with the rice, start rolling it with the guide of a bamboo roller. After one complete rotation, release the roller and finish it off using your hand. Gently but tightly press to make a good roll.

SERVES 3 TO 4

Potato Patties

Gamja-buchim

In Korea, my mother would hike up the trails on the mountainside with her friends in the spring. On the passage up the mountain, there were food stalls where the people could stop and rest while they snacked. Potato patties were my mom's favorite. She remembers how the stall keeper would vigorously shave the potato to get crumbled-up bits. As the shaved bits of potato soaked in water, the potato would bruise in color to a dull brown. The potato patty may not have looked appetizing, but it tasted delicious. My mother learned the recipe and now uses a food processor. She uses a fine-mesh strainer to allow the natural juices from the potato grind to drip out before she molds the patties and cooks them in a hot frying pan.

These potato patties are meant to be a little oily—that's part of what makes them taste so good.

4 IDAHO POTATOES
VEGETABLE OIL
A FEW FRESH WATERCRESS SPRIGS FOR GARNISH

dipping sauce:

2 TEASPOONS SOY SAUCE	1 TEASPOON SESAME SEEDS
½ TEASPOON RED PEPPER FLAKES	½ TEASPOON RICE VINEGAR

1. Peel and clean potatoes. Using a food processor, chop into little pieces. Grind until the consistency is smooth with a grainy texture like a pear. Using a fine-mesh strainer, pour the potato batter through to strain the excess water.

2. Heat oil in a frying pan over a medium flame. Spread the batter into a neat and thick patty about 2 inches in diameter. Cut off a sprig of watercress and embed in the potato while it cooks on the bottom. Do not turn over over to cook the other side until the bottom edges seem brown and caked enough to flip.

3. Combine all the ingredients to make dipping sauce, stir, and serve it on the side with the potato patties. Serve immediately and eat while they're hot!

SERVES 3 TO 4

감자부침

Kimchi Pancakes

Kimchi buchim

1½ CUPS ALL-PURPOSE FLOUR
½ CUP WATER
1 EGG
2 TEASPOONS CRUSHED GARLIC
10 OUNCES KIMCHI, PREFERABLY AGED, CHOPPED INTO SMALL
  PIECES
¼ CUP KIMCHI JUICE
4 OUNCES SCALLIONS, FINELY MINCED USING THE GREENER
  PARTS
2 GREEN CHILI PEPPERS, MINCED
VEGETABLE OIL FOR COOKING

dipping sauce:
2 TEASPOONS SOY SAUCE
½ TEASPOON RED PEPPER FLAKES
1 TEASPOON SESAME SEEDS
½ TEASPOON RICE VINEGAR

1. Combine the flour with water and egg and mix. Add the garlic, kimchi and its juice, scallions, and peppers. Using 1 teaspoon vegetable oil, cook one thin pancake at a time over a medium flame. The batter will make 4 pancakes.

2. Combine all the ingredients for dipping sauce and serve on the side with the kimchi pancakes.

SERVES 3 TO 4

김치부침

Seafood Pancake

Hey-mul pajun

It is said that because Korea was almost all surrounded by water, Koreans looked seaward for culinary inspiration. Hey-mul pajun, a simple and reliable treat, is a good example of this. My parents both spoke of this dish when I was growing up. My father ate it when his family had little to eat, and still to this day he enjoys it with a bottle of soju (sweet potato vodka). My mother told me that the aroma of the dish was so good, that it would entice her neighborhood girlfriends to peek over the walls that divided the homes and ask, "Hey can I come eat that with you?" And because the girls enjoyed the company as much as the food, they sat by the fire cooking up one pancake at a time, talking and eating until their mothers called them back home.

7 OUNCES FRESH SQUID (CALAMARI)

18 OUNCES FRESH SHRIMP

2 OUNCES OYSTERS

2 CUPS FLOUR

1½ CUPS WATER

2 EGGS

2 TEASPOONS CRUSHED GARLIC

½ TEASPOON SALT

5 OUNCES SCALLIONS, CHOPPED INTO 1-INCH PIECES

2 TEASPOONS VEGETABLE OIL

dipping sauce:

2 TEASPOONS SOY SAUCE

2 TABLESPOONS VINEGAR

1 TEASPOON SUGAR

1 TEASPOON RED PEPPER FLAKES

2 TEASPOONS SESAME SEEDS

1. Clean all seafood and slice thin. Keep aside.

2. In mixing bowl, combine the flour, water, and eggs, and with hands, mix in a massaging motion. Then add the shrimp, squid, garlic, and

salt, and with hands, delicately make 5 full rotations to mix in these ingredients to the batter.

3. Add the oysters and scallions and make 5 more delicate rotations with hands.

4. Over a medium flame, heat ½ teaspoon of oil in a frying pan. Then in heated pan, spread the batter, thinly covering the whole pan. Heat until egg is cooked. Continue this step until all batter is used.

5. Prepare the dipping sauce by mixing in all the ingredients in a medium bowl. Serve the seafood pancake cut in manageable sizes for the dipping sauce.

SERVES 3 TO 4

Fish Patties

Seng-sun jun

Fish patties were a favorite after-school snack. My mother would greet us and say, "You must be hungry, let's eat." And in the kitchen were cooked fish patties in a frying pan, covered with a lid. My mother would eat one as we devoured the rest. She purposely never made too many, because she didn't want us to ruin our appetite for dinner. If only dinner could have been fish patties too. . . .

These are good as a snack, or as a ban-chan with rice and kimchi. They are also very tasty in a sandwich with fresh greens and a light cream dressing.

1 POUND FLOUNDER FILLET
2 TABLESPOONS SIFTED FLOUR
2 EGGS
4 OUNCES ONION, JUICED IN A BLENDER
2 TABLESPOONS MINCED SCALLIONS
2 TABLESPOONS CRUSHED GARLIC
½ TEASPOON BLACK PEPPER
½ TEASPOON FINE SALT
VEGETABLE OIL FOR GREASING PAN

1. Mince the flounder, then tenderize it by beating it with the dull side of a knife until the fish is fluffed up.

2. Place the fish in a mixing bowl. Add the flour, eggs, and onion juice and mix together, using your hands to distribute the ingredients evenly. Add the garlic, scallions, black pepper, and salt and thoroughly mix in the seasonings. Form the patties into 2-inch circles; don't make them too thick because they will cook unevenly.

3. Cook the patties in a greased frying pan.

SERVES 2

생선전

Fried Squid Finger Food

Ojinx-o teegim

½ POUND SQUID, CUT INTO 2-INCH STRIPS
¼ CUP WATER
1 CUP WHEAT FLOUR
1 EGG
¼ CUP ONION JUICE
PINCH OF SALT
VEGETABLE OIL FOR FRYER

dipping sauce:
2 TEASPOONS SOY SAUCE
½ TEASPOON RED PEPPER FLAKES
1 TEASPOON SESAME SEEDS
½ TEASPOON RICE VINEGAR

1. In a mixing bowl, combine the water, flour, egg, onion juice, and a pinch of salt and mix together using a fork.

2. Take a squid strip and coat with some flour, then dip into the batter and gently shake off excess.

3. In a fryer, heat oil to about 350 degrees. Cook the squid strips. Lay on paper towels for the excess oil to be absorbed.

4. Combine ingredients for dipping sauce and serve on the side with the fried squid.

SERVES 2 TO 3

오징어 튀김

Spicy Squid Salad

Ojinx-o moochim

1½ POUNDS SQUID, CLEANED AND GUTTED, CUT INTO GENEROUS
    PIECES ABOUT 1 X 1½ INCHES
½ POUND SPINACH
HANDFUL OF CHOPPED CABBAGE
HANDFUL OF THINLY SLICED ZUCCHINI
HANDFUL OF CHOPPED SCALLIONS

sauce:
4 TABLESPOONS SOY SAUCE
2 TABLESPOONS RICE VINEGAR
1 TABLESPOON CRUSHED GARLIC
2 TABLESPOONS RED PEPPER SAUCE
1 TEASPOON RED PEPPER FLAKES
1 TEASPOON SESAME SALT
2 TABLESPOONS SESAME OIL
2 TABLESPOONS BROWN SUGAR

1. Prepare the vegetables. Blanch the spinach by itself, and the cabbage, zucchini, and scallion together. Strain. For the spinach, wring out the water using your hands. Put the vegetables aside.

2. In a large mixing bowl, stir together all the ingredients for the sauce. Keep aside.

3. Prepare squid. Bring 5 cups of water to a boil, over a high flame. To keep it soft, blanch the squid for 2 to 3 minutes while stirring. Strain immediately and combine the squid and the vegetables in the mixing bowl with the sauce. Toss together using a spoon or fork. Serve immediately.

SERVES 3 TO 4

오징어 무침

As children, we all have moments in our lives when we think that our mom is the best, and how lucky we are to have such a great mom. Her unconditional love for us was expressed in many ways, but especially through her cooking. Every year in school, there were cultural events where all the students would have to bring in a different dish as a way of sharing their ethnic roots. Like most of the other Korean moms, Mom would usually make kimbop, but hers was the always the best—the feeling was unanimous. Her plate of kimbop always vanished first. One year, instead of kimbop, she made her fried-squid finger food for the school fair. The plate of squid didn't last half an hour. As I sat behind the table of food, the hardest thing for me to do was to keep from eating all the squid myself. Hearing everyone rave about how great my mother's cooking was during moments like this made me proud and made me realize how truly wonderful my mother really is.

—Moon Sun Kwak

Beef-Stuffed Chili Peppers

Gogi gochu-buchim

Having anjou to snack on while toasting with shots of sweet potato vodka, my parents sometimes played hatto, a Korean poker game. With much excitement, a plate of this beef in chili pepper was passed around the table. While the grown-ups played their card game, my sisters and I would sneak a few of these spicy treats, wandering around the table, trying to figure out how the game was played. Eventually, of course, we were asked to play in the other room so that the grown-ups could concentrate on poker (and anjou).

8 MEDIUM-SIZE KOREAN GREEN
   CHILI PEPPERS
10 OUNCES LEAN BEEF
1 TABLESPOON SOY SAUCE
1 TABLESPOON SESAME OIL
1 TABLESPOON CRUSHED GARLIC

1 TEASPOON SUGAR
1 TEASPOON RICE WINE (SAKE)
PINCH OF BLACK PEPPER
2 EGGS
FLOUR
VEGETABLE OIL

1. Halve the cleaned chili peppers and remove seeds. Keep aside.

2. Mince the beef and beat with the blunt side of your knife until the beef feels even and soft in texture.

3. In a mixing bowl, season the beef with soy sauce, sesame oil, crushed garlic, sugar, rice wine, and black pepper and massage in using your hands. Roll the beef to be stuffed in the chili pepper, using your hands to fit the pepper neatly. Before you stuff the chili pepper, shake in some flour in the interior of the chili pepper. This helps the beef to bind in the pepper when it is being cooked. Do this to all the halved chili peppers, then stuff with beef.

4. Beat the eggs together in a bowl suitable for dipping the stuffed peppers. Doing this one at a time, gently cover the stuffed pepper with a light coat of flour, then coat with egg, allowing the excess to trickle off.

5. Using a shallow frying pan, heat the vegetable oil and pan-fry the stuffed peppers. Adding a little oil as you go along, cook the peppers as you batter them. Serve on a platter in a neat arrangement.

SERVES 2 TO 3

Spicy Beef and Vegetable Salad

Gogi-moochim

1 POUND BEEF SATAY (SEE PAGE 5), CUT INTO 2 CHUNKS
HANDFUL OF MUNGBEAN SPROUTS
½ POUND SPINACH
HANDFUL OF CHOPPED CABBAGE
HANDFUL OF CHOPPED ONION
HANDFUL OF CHOPPED SCALLIONS
HANDFUL OF THINLY SLICED ZUCCHINI

sauce:
4 TABLESPOONS SOY SAUCE
1 TEASPOON RED PEPPER FLAKES
1 TABLESPOON VINEGAR
1 TABLESPOON BROWN SUGAR
1 TABLESPOON CRUSHED GARLIC
1 TEASPOON HOT MUSTARD, OR MORE IF YOU DESIRE THE DISH
    SPICIER
2 TABLESPOONS SESAME OIL
1 TABLESPOON SESAME SALT

1. Using 6 cups of water, cook the beef over a medium flame for 20 minutes. Reduce the flame to low and cook for 20 more minutes. Poke to see if the beef is well cooked. If the fork or chopstick goes through smoothly, the beef is done. Strain and allow it to cool entirely at room temperature. Slice the beef into generous pieces about ¼ inch thick. Keep aside.

2. Prepare the vegetables. All the vegetables need to be blanched. Blanch the spinach separately from the other vegetables. Drain. For the spinach, squeeze out excess water using your hands.

3. In a mixing bowl, stir together the ingredients for the sauce, then add the vegetables and beef. Toss together using a spoon or fork. Serve at room temperature.

SERVES 2 TO 3

Refreshments and Treats
(Gamjou)

감주

Having fresh fruit after dinner was a routine pleasure. My father brought home fresh fruit by the case. We ate Korean melons and pears, or sugar-sprinkled strawberries, watermelon, and grapes for dessert in the summer or roasted chestnuts and tangerines in the winter.

When our mother put out a bowl of fresh cherries for us, my sister Moon Sun had a funny habit of fetching a small saucer from the kitchen to reserve the best-looking cherries for herself. She looked for the most plump and ruby red cherries and would not share them with us. My mother watched her in astonishment and told her to share. She reassured Moon Sun that she would buy her plenty more. My sister would kick and holler until her face turned red if I tried to eat one of the cherries in her bowl. She saved the cherries to eat later if she could not finish them in one sitting. She was five years old. "Which genes did she inherit," my mother would ask my father, "to make her behave so strangely?"

Fresh fruit, and the following recipes, are delicious enough to make a person act strangely indeed.

Sweet Rice-Malt Drink

Shi'ke

You will need a rice cooker that holds 8 to 12 servings to make this drink.

1 POUND MALT FLOUR, COARSE FLAKES
1 CUP RICE
1 CUP SUGAR

1. Combine 1 gallon of water with the malt flour. Remove the particles of floating malt using a fine-mesh strainer, or by cupping it with your hand, and discard. Allow the malt to soak in the water until the water gets cloudy, 5 to 6 hours. Use a fine-mesh strainer to separate the malt flour from the water. Save the cloudy water to make the drink but discard the malt.

2. Using a rice cooker, combine rice with ¾ cup of water and cook. After 25 to 30 minutes, the rice should be cooked.

3. Gently pour the malt water into the rice cooker with the cooked rice. If there are any more floating particles of malt, discard them. Stir 2 tablespoons of sugar into the malt water and rice in the rice cooker. Leave the contents on "warm" for 5 hours in the rice cooker. By now the body of the rice grain should be dissolved and the rice bits should appear in flat pieces.

4. Transfer the contents in the rice cooker to a pot and boil once with the rest of the sugar mixed in. Chill. Garnish with pine nuts before serving.

SERVES 10 TO 15

As a little girl in Korea, my mother ate persimmons and there is a folktale that explains why this fruit appeals to the children there: A mean tiger roamed the mountainsides of Korea during the cold months of winter looking for prey. When he could not find food in the stretch of mountains covered in snow, he searched the village nearby to find something to eat. One day, a small child's cry lured the tiger closer to a house where a woman was trying to lull her baby to sleep. The tiger crouched by the house, planning his attack, and listened for them outside the door.

"There, there baby. If you don't stop crying, the fox will come and get you," the mother said as the baby kept crying.

"There, there, if you really don't stop crying, a wolf will come and get you!" said the mother, lulling the baby in her arms. The baby cried even louder; he was not afraid of the fox or the wolf. The tiger that was listening outside thought: how strange for this child to not be afraid of being eaten by the fox or the wolf. All children are afraid of them! The tiger was confused.

"There, there baby. Stop crying because there is a tiger waiting outside to come and get you if you don't stop crying this minute!" the mother said to the baby, who kept crying. The baby was not afraid of the tiger either.

The tiger was startled—how do they know I'm here? And why is the baby still crying, is he not afraid of me? Am I not the scariest animal? The tiger grew furious and was about to roar, when he heard the mother say, "There, there baby, stop crying! Here is the dried persimmon!" The baby stopped crying and there was silence in the room.

Puzzled, the tiger backed away from the house. "Is a persimmon an animal, much bigger and more horrifying than I?" the tiger thought and became fearful and fled from the house. He was terrified that he would be eaten by a persimmon! The tiger did not know the baby stopped crying because the mother gave the child a delicious treat. What a foolish tiger!

Ginger and Cinnamon Punch

Sujong-gwa

Traditionally, ginger and cinnamon punch is served on New Year's Day after an extravagant meal. This is how my mother remembers it being served. The punch is very sweet—a real treat for children. After New Year's, the leftover punch would be chilled out in the cold. The children would help themselves to more punch until it was gone and always looked forward to the next New Year's to have it again.

½ POUND NATURAL CINNAMON CRACKED INTO PIECES
4 OUNCES GINGERROOT, SLICED
1 CUP BROWN SUGAR

garnish:
PINE NUTS
DRIED PERSIMMONS, SOAKED IN WATER FOR ABOUT 30 MINUTES

1. In a heavy pot, combine the cinnamon and ginger with 12 cups of water and cook for 30 minutes. Then lower the flame and simmer for 15 more minutes. Scoop out the ginger and cinnamon particles using a fine-mesh strainer with a handle. While it is still hot, mix in the brown sugar. Allow it to chill.

2. When ready to serve, garnish with 1 persimmon per serving and some pine nuts. This punch should be served in a low, round, ceramic bowl for the full traditional effect.

SERVES 10 TO 15

Chestnut Treats

Bam gaang-jong

½ POUND CHESTNUTS
1 TABLESPOON TOASTED SESAME SEEDS
⅓ TEASPOON SALT
2 TABLESPOONS HONEY
⅛ CUP PINE NUTS

1. Boil whole chestnuts in 2 cups of water over a medium flame for 40 minutes. Cool chestnuts by running them under water. When the chestnuts cool completely, they are easier to peel.

2. Using a mortar and pestle, grind the chestnuts to mush. Add the sesame seeds and grind together. In a mixing bowl, combine the salt, honey, chestnuts, and sesame seeds. Make into a ball. In a food processor, grind the pine nuts to a coarse powder. Roll the chestnut balls in it for a thin and even coat.

SERVES 2 TO 3

밤
강
정

Ginger Treats

Pyun-gaang

Ginger treats are favored for many reasons. They are good to eat for stomach pains, appetite loss, and for motion sickness. My mother craved these spicy treats when she was pregnant. Both men and women also like these ginger treats as anjou, *with complementing pieces of toasted squid or cuttlefish, peanuts, and raw chestnuts.*

4 OUNCES FRESH GINGERROOT
1 CUP SUGAR
½ TEASPOON SALT

1. Clean (but do not unpeel) ginger and thinly slice. Blanch ginger in boiling water. Keep aside.

2. In a pan, combine ⅓ cup of the sugar and the salt with ⅓ cup of water. Stir thoroughly and add the ginger pieces. Cook over a medium flame for 7 to 10 minutes, stirring, until all the water evaporates.

3. Use the remaining sugar to coat the ginger. Take individual pieces of ginger to coat them evenly with sugar, then allow to dry on a flat surface. When dry, they are ready to eat. The outside should crust and the inside should be chewy and soft.

SERVES 6 TO 7

편
강

Index